LESSON
STUDY
Communities

LESSON STUDY
Communities

**Increasing Achievement
With Diverse Students**

KARIN WIBURG   SUSAN BROWN

Foreword by Akihiko Takahashi

CORWIN PRESS
A SAGE Publications Company
Thousand Oaks, CA 91320

For information:

Corwin Press
A Sage Publications Company
2455 Teller Road
Thousand Oaks, California 91320
www.corwinpress.com

Sage Publications Ltd.
1 Oliver's Yard
55 City Road
London EC1Y 1SP
United Kingdom

Sage Publications India Pvt. Ltd.
B-42, Panchsheel Enclave
Post Box 4109
New Delhi 110 017 India

Printed in the United States of America

Library of Congress Cataloging-in-Publication Data

Wiburg, Karin M.
Lesson study communities: Increasing achievement with diverse students/Karin Wiburg, Susan Brown.
     p. cm.
Includes bibliographical references and index.
ISBN 1-4129-1644-5 (cloth) — ISBN 1-4129-1645-3 (pbk.)
   1. Lesson planning—Study and teaching. 2. Teachers—Inservice training. 3. Curriculum planning—Study and teaching. 4. Multicultural education—Study and teaching. I. Brown, Susan (Susan W.) II. Title.
LB1027.4.W554 2007
375.'001-dc22   2006002894

This book is printed on acid-free paper.

06   07   08   09   10   9   8   7   6   5   4   3   2   1

Acquisitions Editor:	Rachel Livsey
Editorial Assistant:	Phyllis Cappello
Copy Editor:	Bill Bowers
Typesetter:	C&M Digitals (P) Ltd.
Indexer:	Sylvia Coates
Cover Designer:	Michael Dubowe

Contents

Foreword

I have a clear memory of the blue sky, the horizon over the desert, and the straightaway to the Mexican border that led me to the school. The school overlooked the stunning mountain scenery across the desert. With only sand and a few buildings around the school, it looked very different from the schools in Chicago where I regularly visited to observe lessons.

It was February 2004, my first visit to a school in New Mexico. My purpose was to help teachers there conduct their first public research lesson along with my colleagues from the New Mexico MathStar project. I had had several opportunities before to hear about the MathStar project's efforts to improve the teaching and learning of mathematics by using lesson study, but it was my first time to be an actual part of their lesson study endeavor.

After we walked into the school, several other educators from local school districts joined us to participate in a public research lesson. We observed a mathematics research lesson in which a teacher and his students used both English and Spanish to communicate with each other. During the participants' discussion, which was held right after the research lesson, members of the team that had planned the lesson talked about their experience of collaborating with each other. I was moved when I heard a team member emphasize that her lesson study endeavor had been highly rewarding because she had never experienced such collaboration with her colleagues before. At the same time, I recognized that the lesson planning team had successfully established a lesson study foundation and was ready to move toward the second stage.

Lesson study, which originated in Japan, has played an important role in Japanese teachers' professional development since Japanese public education started more than a hundred years ago. In contrast, U.S. educators have only recently become interested in lesson study as a promising source of ideas for improving education. In 2000, there were only a few places in the U.S. where researchers and practitioners worked together trying to implement lesson study. The New Mexico MathStar project was one of these pioneers of lesson study.

My own lesson study journey with U.S. educators began in the summer of 2000 in Tokyo, where a couple of lesson study workshops were held for U.S. researchers and educators. One year later, a group of California teachers and researchers asked me to help them implement lesson study in their schools. I demonstrated a research lesson so they could actually experience lesson study, and afterwards I met a couple of members from the New Mexico MathStar project at a conference. That was the first time I learned that teachers and researchers in New Mexico had been trying to use lesson study to improve their mathematics teaching and learning.

Years later, when I visited the first public research lesson in New Mexico, which I described in my opening paragraphs, I was impressed to find that the project had begun to establish a foundation of lesson study in less than a couple of years. It impressed me because, through my participation in the lesson study activities of other pioneers, I have learned that the process of implementing lesson study in U.S. schools has not been smooth.

Karin Miller Wiburg and Susan W. Brown, the authors of this book, played key roles in the New Mexico MathStar project, which U.S. lesson study researchers and practitioners have recognized as one of the successful pioneers of lesson study in the U.S. Since the inception of the New Mexico initiative, the authors have worked closely with teachers and educators in New Mexico to find ways to implement lesson study in schools where most students have been underserved. As their book makes clear, the authors are aware of the challenges of implementing lesson study in a U.S. school, and they try to avoid transplanting lesson study in a superficial way. They carefully analyze similarities and differences between Japanese lesson study and existing professional development approaches in the U.S. And they try to capture how the philosophical background of lesson study relates to other approaches.

Also, due to the authors' effort, this book does not limit itself simply to describing the process of implementing lesson study in the schools of New Mexico. The chapters provide a broad look at the implementation of lesson study in the U.S. This perspective helps us to develop a notion that implementing lesson study is a way to provide important ingredients that are missing from U.S. school environments rather than a new approach to replace existing professional development.

If you are seeking a more effective way to improve teaching and learning for your students, seeking a way to collaborate with your colleagues to improve your school, or seeking innovative ways to help your teachers become actively involved in their professional career, you will learn from the work of Karin Wiburg and Susan Brown.

— *Akihiko Takahashi*

Preface

The purpose of this book is to share our work in building lesson study communities in the United States, how we created successful lesson study models, the many barriers we encountered and mostly overcame, and how you might want to use lesson study to address learning problems in your own schools. The work should be especially useful for two reasons. The results of lesson study over the last 5 years include demonstrated success in using lesson study for enhancing teacher quality and improving student learning and accomplishment. Descriptions of how we achieved this success are woven throughout the book. The second unique feature is that the lesson study teachers and students with whom we have worked come from among the most poorly served schools and communities in the United States. As Linda Darling has written, poor schools often have the newest and most inexperienced teachers with the least professional development.

The successful use of an unusually rich kind of teacher-directed professional development with primarily Hispanic and Native American teachers and students in poor communities, and the resulting success of their students, bode well for the use of lesson study and its possible modifications for addressing a currently pressing problem—how to close the achievement gap. Ethnically and linguistically diverse students have remained at the bottom in achievement in the United States. However, recently released results of a new state-required, criterion-referenced test in New Mexico show that fourth graders in the 95 percent Hispanic and low-income Gadsden district scored as well, on average, as all fourth graders in the state. Further, a recently completed National Science Foundation (NSF) study—examining possible connections between teacher professional development and student achievement— showed that the most significant predictor of students' achievement is whether or not their teachers had been involved in collaborative lesson and curriculum planning (Wiburg, 2005).

It is worth noting that the ways in which we conduct lesson study in the United States are grounded in a culturally responsive approach to teaching and curriculum that particularly addresses the challenges schools face as a result of the changed demographics of their students. We are dedicated to providing expanded learning opportunities for all students, especially those who still remain behind. Our work has been successful in many ways in addition to those recently reported in 2005 test data.

- An outside evaluator involved in the initial MathStar project reported that all teachers in the project reported expanding their teaching strategies to involve more students.
- Increases in mathematics test scores are also being reported for students whose teachers participated in lesson study. For example, in one dual-language elementary school located near the Mexican border, 76 percent of the elementary school students scored at or above proficiency in mathematics in 2004. (This competence was far above the state average for both Hispanic and Anglo/White students,which is around 50 percent.)
- Middle school students in a 98 percent Hispanic border school district with large numbers of English Language Learners have raised their mathematics achievement from 1999 (when only 8 percent of middle school students demonstrated proficiency in mathematics) to around 40 percent of the students in this school being at or above mathematics proficiency in 2004.

Why lesson study? First of all, it is based on an understanding that teaching and learning are cultural activities (Stigler & Hiebert, 1999). We believe that only by addressing the culture of teaching and learning will we be able to change the system in such a way that many more children succeed in school. There have been many efforts to reform mathematics and science education. However, the achievement gap in many cases remains the same. It is important to recognize that math and science classrooms have not always been perceived as engaging and exciting learning environments by non-mainstream children. Perhaps more important, teachers have not been fully included in educational reform efforts and have not been assisted in thinking about what students are learning or not learning from their teaching. Successful reform focuses on what teachers and students are expected to do in classrooms, and lesson study, with its focus on student learning, is an ideal model of professional development for educators interesting in improving student achievement. Change, in order to be successful, must be driven by teachers and based on instructional decisions. What at first appears to be a slow educational reform process—the involvement of teachers in substantial study of their students, their lessons, and their students' learning—may turn out to be one of the most effective ways to reenergize learning in classrooms.

For us, the decision to introduce lesson study grew out of our frustration during the second year of the implementation of a mathematics reform grant, when the work we had been doing seemed to be making no changes in classrooms. Even though teachers in this initiative had attended two summer institutes and evaluated them highly, we were seeing no changes in practice when visiting classrooms. We found no changes in the way teachers were teaching or students were learning mathematics, even when we thought we had taught them the tools and strategies we thought they needed to improve mathematics learning.

During the spring of 2001, we read Stigler and Hiebert's (1999) book *The Teaching Gap,* which illuminated the differences in the culture of teaching mathematics in Japanese classrooms as compared to American classrooms. The book is based on the international TIMMS study, which compared student performance in mathematics in the United States, Germany, and Japan. The TIMMS study captured, through video, the differences in teaching in these countries, and the authors concluded that the differences in teaching cultures within a country were far less than between countries. Stigler and Hiebert (1999) introduced the professional development form most used by elementary mathematics teachers in Japan, which has been translated as lesson study. In Japanese, this term means a teacher-led investigation of how the lesson went, what students were still having trouble learning, and how the lesson could be modified to improve learning.

In spring 2000, we decided we were no longer going to "do things to teachers," and from this point forward our staff and faculty committed to co-constructing professional development with teachers. The problems we would address would be "our problems" and we would find the solutions to students' learning difficulties together. The following is a quick overview of the chapters in this book. When appropriate, the voices of leaders and teachers involved in the practice of lesson study are introduced in order to make this work as rich as possible. Each chapter ends with some questions designed to extend the reader's understanding of the chapter's concepts. These extended learning exercises are intended for use by groups of teachers and/or administrators who are reading this material together. These questions can be discussed in person or by using a bulletin board or a discussion space on the Web.

Chapter 1, Translating Lesson Study From Japan to the United States, introduces lesson study as it began in Japan and has since been introduced in the United States. Some of the common barriers to doing lesson study in this country are described. Principles that address the solutions to these barriers through well-grounded lesson study are introduced, with the aim of building a framework for the practice of lesson study in schools in this country.

Chapter 2, Building Successful Lesson Study Communities, describes the initial MathStar model and then introduces several different types of successful lesson study communities. Because of some of the differences between Japanese education and the diversity of American education—as well as the diverse communities it serves—differences in the types of lesson study communities have emerged naturally over the last few years. These communities include teachers involved in state or multistate grant projects; whole-district or whole-school lesson study; lesson study as it might be used to integrate content learning and teaching; and the development of lesson study by teachers for their own teaching. This chapter also suggests how lesson study can be empowering to teachers and students working in bilingual or multilingual classrooms. The chapter closes with a description of lesson study as used in a largely Hispanic U.S.-Mexico border district.

Chapter 3, Assessing Your Readiness for Lesson Study, introduces ways to consider whether you and/or your school are ready for lesson study. A desire to begin doing lesson study sometimes occurs from the need to simply do things differently, because what you have been doing in terms of increasing student achievement has not been working. Occasionally, lesson study is introduced in a top-down fashion, and at other times it emerges from teacher work at the grassroots level. Traditionally, lesson study advocates have said that it is important for teachers to introduce this process. Yet, in some of our examples, lesson study succeeds even when introduced in a top-down fashion and then followed up by providing teachers opportunities to develop ownership of their work. This chapter articulates a set of threshold conditions in schools, which can contribute to a successful lesson study program. Lesson study by itself is not a magic bullet and cannot change student learning without a schoolwide effort to also align teaching, assessment, and the use of quality materials with high-level content standards.

Chapter 4, Connecting Instructional Goals to Lesson Study, is organized around teacher groups engaging in processes that ensure lesson study is connected to each school's and/or district's educational aims and instructional goals. Most schools, faced with the high stakes involved in accountability pressures, can't afford to try new forms of professional development if they are not directly connected to each school's learner-based improvement plans. What connects a school's plan for improvement to teachers' professional development is the use of an overarching goal, which guides the work of every teacher group. Even though teams may be at different grade levels or work at opposite ends of the state or nation, they need to find a way to develop for themselves an inclusive overarching goal. There are also subgoals that need to be developed related to content, units, and research lessons. These subgoals relate to what kinds of people we want our students to become; to what learning strategies are appropriate in the discipline being learned; and to what we want students to know and be able to do as a result of the units taught. The beauty of lesson study is that the teachers, who are responsible for the implementation of improvements in instruction, are also responsible for creating these goals and the ways in which they can be met in the classroom. The process for doing this is explained in Chapter 4.

Chapter 5, Designing the Research Lesson, provides example cases around teacher team building during the lesson study process, as well as documents the support required for getting started by using specific templates and assistance from outside experts. The research lesson is a window into the work that teachers are doing to improve student learning. Groups of teachers collaboratively plan a lesson that is carefully designed to answer specific questions about student thinking and learning. The lesson is taught by one of the group members and observed by the others. After the lesson, the group convenes to discuss the observation and its effectiveness in meeting their goals. They revise the lesson based on their learning, and the lesson is taught a second time. The format of the research lesson is not typical of U.S. classroom instruction. Special attention must be given to student thinking, teacher responses, and data collection. The research lesson should not be confused with traditional individual teacher lesson planning.

Chapter 6, Reflecting on and Sharing Your Research Lesson, illustrates how the lesson study process is most successful, both for individual teachers and teacher groups, when the lesson study process includes a public sharing of lessons learned. Many teachers are not used to seeing themselves as professional researchers who can contribute to improvements in education. Nor are they used to working collaboratively with other teachers in order to build knowledge about teaching and learning. Care must be taken when it comes to understanding the level of intensity required by lesson study. An experienced mentor can help teacher groups and schools to move through what is often initially a frustrating process. Some questions to be considered are: How many members are too many? Can a team span grade and subject levels? Should team members all be located at the same school? How can teachers learn to be critical friends in terms of practice, while still remaining respectful of each other? There is also the issue of group working practices and the facilitation of communication.

During this sharing phase, teachers "consolidate the learning" that occurred during earlier stages and take a professional step in organizing this learning in a way that can be demonstrated and shared with other members of the education community. This sharing may take the form of demonstration lessons, conference presentations, and/or research reports, and can be done on a schoolwide, districtwide, or state or national basis.

Chapter 7, Integrating Lesson Study With Existing School Initiatives, responds to the common problem of how difficult it is to add anything new to the already overcrowded curriculum and the daily work of teachers and administrators. The chapter includes three models that have been used to integrate lesson study into existing school initiatives and describes how implementing lesson study in the United States can strengthen already ongoing work for improving student achievement. Examples are provided that suggest how to begin lesson study and lessen the possible resistance to change that might occur in school communities. These models are explored in depth in this chapter, concluding with such practical information as the people and processes required for each approach.

The Resources can be used to help you implement Lesson Study in your school. They include an example of a problem-based lesson; specific and detailed guidelines for steps of the lesson study; and professional development workshop guidelines.

Acknowledgments

The original group who introduced lesson study in New Mexico consisted of an education professor, Karin Wiburg, a doctoral student in mathematics, Jeff Hovermill Samatha, three math professional development specialists (Wanda Guzman, Lisa Snow, and Cathy Kinzer), and a technical team (Kalle Joregensen and Jennifer Villa), who had received training in videography from the Lesson Lab Group. Kalle videotaped the lessons, teacher interactions, and inverviews, while Jennifer provided the Web-based support necessary to do lesson study at a distance in the rural Southwest. Other professional development experts at our university and in school districts soon extended lesson study beyond mathematics learning into their own work in science (Susan Brown); bilingual education (Rocio Benedicto and David Rutledge); and as an integral part of a statewide technology integration movement (Susan Bussmann and Karen Trujillo). Over the past 2 years, as part of a new Math Science Partnership (MSP) grant, eight university mathematicians have joined our learning group and helped to integrate a deep understanding of content with pedagogy. This book is dedicated to the New Mexico Learning Collaborative, the professors and teachers who are committed to providing the diverse students of the Southwest with the best possible learning opportunities. It is also dedicated to the 24 original math teachers throughout New Mexico, in tiny towns and larger cities, who decided to give this process a try in 2001, as well as the more than 250 teachers who have worked with us over the last 6 years.

Contributing Authors

We would like to thank the following members of our group who wrote additional material that has enriched this book:

- Jeff Hovermill Samatha is currently a mathematics professor at Northern Arizona University, who is continuing his lesson study work in Arizona, including work with Navaho teachers. He is the primary author of Chapter 6, on extending and sharing lesson study.
- Susan Bussmann and Karen Trujillo, project directors of recent lesson study projects, contributed practical models for integrating lesson study with other school reforms in Chapter 7.
- David Rutledge, an assistant professor of curriculum and learning technologies at NMSU, and Rocio Benedicto, who coordinates programs for Latino families and students, contributed information in Chapter 2 on how lesson study could help bilingual teachers and students.

Additional Acknowledgments

Thanks to Stacey Duncan and Liz Parra Kriegel for final editing and formatting. Appreciation to Frannie Dever, mathematics district expert, who made lesson study the form of professional development in the Albuquerque schools.

Thanks also to two principals, Cindy Chapman and Sharon Duncan, in the Albuquerque and Gadsden schools, respectively, who made their institutions whole-school lesson study schools. A special thanks to Akahiko Takahashi, who agreed to write the Foreword and who has helped us with lesson study several times over the years, including helping us with our first public lesson in a 95 percent Hispanic school district.

Corwin Press gratefully acknowledges the contributions of the following reviewers:

Gail Derrick
Associate Professor
Regent University
Virginia Beach, VA

Jenny Sue Flannagan
Elementary Science Coordinator
Virginia Beach City Public Schools
Virginia Beach, VA

Antonette W. Hood
Assistant Professor
California State University, San Marcos
San Marcos, CA

Thelma A. Davis
Coordinator, K–12 Mathematics and Science
Clark County School District
Las Vegas, NV

Patricia B. Schwartz
Principal
Thomas Jefferson Middle School
Teaneck, NJ

Catherine Lewis
Distinguished Research Scholar
Mills College
Oakland, CA

Sonal Chokshi
Director of Lesson Study
Community Outreach
San Jose, CA

Vernet C. Nettles
Education Specialist
Alabama State Department of Education
Montgomery, AL

Clea Fernandez
Teachers College–Columbia University
New York, NY

Kathy DiRanna
K–12 Alliance Statewide Director
WestEd
Santa Ana, CA

Pam Hankins
Staff Development Specialist
Springfield Public Schools
Springfield, MO

About the Authors

 **Karin M. Wiburg** is Associate Dean for Research at New Mexico State University, and continues to spend one-quarter of her time conducting research into mathematics education and closing the achievement gap on the border. She has been a professor of curriculum and learning technologies in the C&I Department in the College of Education at NMSU since 1993. Prior to that, she taught in higher education in California and served as Coordinator of the Technology Consortium at the San Diego County Office. She also spent 13 years as a teacher and administrator in the Seattle public schools in areas related to math, technology, and reading.

She has been involved in distance education since 1987, when she used an Apple II computer as a SYSOP for a teacher network in California. At NMSU since 1993, she has coordinated a specialization in learning technologies, which includes distance education programs at the master's and doctoral levels. She has received numerous grants for technology and mathematics and science education, has coauthored three textbooks, and has written numerous articles for publication. She has been a frequent presenter at national conferences and is primarily interested in the improvement of learning environments.

 **Susan W. Brown** is Principal Investigator/ Project Director for several grants, including the Southern New Mexico Science, Engineering, Mathematics, and Aerospace Academy, in the College of Education at New Mexico State University in Las Cruces, New Mexico. Her research focus is science education and the underrepresentation of minority students and females in the fields of science, math,

and engineering, and the grants reflect this focus. Besides the grant work, she teaches early childhood and elementary science methods at New Mexico State University. She also works with NASA as an Aerospace Education Specialist. Throughout her teaching and research career, she has earned numerous awards, such as the 2004 New Mexico State University Outstanding Research Presidential Award for Excellence in Science Teaching, the Disney/McDonald Award, Who's Who Among America's Teachers, and special recognition from the New Mexico legislature. She is nationally board certified and has facilitated many educators' workshops. Dr. Brown has presented and been published both nationally and internationally.

1

Translating Lesson Study From Japan to the United States

Improving something as complex and culturally embedded as teaching requires the efforts of all the players, including students, parents, and politicians. But teachers must be the primary driving force behind change. They are best positioned to understand the problems that students face and to generate possible solutions.

—James Stigler and James Hiebert (1999)

Throughout the history of education, there have been efforts to improve the practice of teaching. One form of professional development that has received considerable public attention lately is lesson study, which originally emerged in Japan after the Second World War. The term *lesson study* was coined by a prominent authority of lesson study, Makoto Yoshida (1999), to describe a collaborative process in which teachers devise a research lesson, teach and observe the lesson, and then revise and reteach the lesson in an iterative cycle of professional learning. Yoshida translated the words "lesson study" from the Japanese term *jugyokenkyu*, which is composed of two words, *jugyo* meaning lesson and *kenkyu* meaning study or research. The lesson study process in Japan is usually a schoolwide effort that takes time and thoughtful collaboration in designing, teaching, observing, and reteaching lessons. The purposes include improving teaching practice as well as curriculum development.

Today lesson study is emerging in the United States as an increasingly popular form of teacher-directed professional development designed to improve mathematics learning, though its use is now expanding beyond mathematics into additional content areas. Many attribute its growth in the U.S. to Stigler and Hiebert's (1999) book *The Teaching Gap,* which suggests that the different cultures of mathematics teaching in Japan and the U.S. help to explain the relatively lower performance of mathematics students in the U.S. (TIMMS, 2003). In the last few years, an increasing number of books and articles have given us an excellent foundation for what lesson study is and how it has been used in Japan (see Fernandez & Yoshida, 2004; Fernandez, 2003; Fernandez & Chokshi, 2002; Lewis, 2002; Lewis & Tsuchida, 1998; National Research Council, 2000a; Takahashi, 2000).

Ironically, lesson study, like two other Japanese reform movements after World War II—Total Quality Management (TQM) and Quality Circles—was heavily influenced by ideas that originated in the United States. All these reform efforts are grounded in the notion of continuous improvements in practice, whether in business or education. Fernandez and Yoshida (2004) report in their excellent book on Japanese lesson study that the concept of problem-solving learning became popular in Japan in the 1920s and 1930s as part of the New Education Movement. Lesson study as it is practiced today in Japan borrows from American ideas related to inquiry learning and a well-established theoretical tradition, which advocates that teachers need to become involved in collaborative action research (Sagor, 1992) and reflective teaching (Connolly & Clandinin, 1992).

A primary reason why lesson study developed naturally as the form of professional development for elementary teachers in Japan is that for many years the Japanese have recognized the power of teachers helping other teachers, and saw teachers as best able to develop the curriculum and lessons to be used in their schools. Japan systematically sent experienced teachers out into rural schools to help new teachers learn how to teach. Due to limited resources for professional development, the system of teachers teaching teachers was well established, though the emphasis on teaching was still traditional for many years (A. Takahashi, personal communication, July 12–30, 2004). Providing teachers the time needed to work with other teachers to design and evaluate lessons is another factor deeply embedded in the culture of schooling in Japan.

Several other factors contributed to the growth of Japanese lesson study. Japan has a national curriculum focused specifically on the big ideas or concepts in each discipline that students must learn at different grade levels. Regarding the mathematics curriculum, Liping Ma (1999) has shown that most Japanese teachers have a fairly deep understanding of mathematics. Because of this understanding they are able to anticipate students' thinking in relation to mathematics tasks, ask appropriate questions, and support the expansion of their thinking in ways required for successful lesson study. In the United States, teachers are often required to take only limited courses in mathematics during their preservice education, and then required by a textbook-driven curriculum to cover a much larger volume of mathematics concepts at a fairly superficial level. Some have referred to the U.S. mathematics curriculum as "a mile wide and an inch deep."

In addition, in the U.S., deep controversies—sometimes known as the "math wars"—exist within the mathematics education community over how math should be taught (for further information, see www.mathematicallycorrect.com). The same is true in reading and other subjects. We have a highly politicized schooling system that supports regional approaches to education. Local school boards make decisions, and districts and state legislatures can delimitate the kinds of curriculum that should be taught in schools both explicitly through local policy and implicitly through state testing and accountability systems.

In contrast, in Japan there is a single curriculum handbook, which covers the key conceptual mathematical ideas students should learn from first through sixth grade and suggests how teachers can help students master these ideas (A. Takahashi, personal communication, July 12–30, 2004). All teachers in Japan accept these key developmental stages of mathematical understanding and then work together, through lesson study, to research and discover the best ways to teach these ideas. These and other differences in the cultural milieu of schooling in Japan and the U.S. need to be understood if we are to design a successful framework for practicing lesson study in the United States.

Lesson Study in the United States

The story of lesson study in the United States began for us through a 5-year professional development grant from the U.S. Department of Education, 1999–2004. This grant funded the MathStar program in three states—California, Colorado, and New Mexico—and was intended to improve middle school mathematics teaching and learning using technology. Each state took a different lead role in the implementation of MathStar. The decision to use lesson study was rooted in our frustration with the results of traditional top-down professional development, in which paid experts lecture or lead teachers through exercises on how to improve their practice.

The Lesson Study Cycle

The following is a brief overview of the general lesson study cycle that we have evolved over the last 4 years. You may notice that many examples in this book feature mathematics content. However, lesson study can also be used in other content areas and is emerging in literacy and science programs, including English Language Learner (ELL) classrooms.

In the following example, teachers work together in teams to consider an area of interest or difficulty in mathematics for their students. The teachers develop student goals, research together the math content, and carefully plan a lesson. The lesson is taught by one of the teachers and observed by the team, who gather data about how the lesson is going. There are various ways to gather data, from scripting what happens in the lesson to asking members of the team to look at different aspects of the lesson, such as how students are interacting, what academic language is being used, and what students seem to understand. Following this observation, which is often videotaped, the group gathers to debrief on what happened and to plan for possible changes in the next cycle of the lesson. The research lesson is then revised through reflection and thoughtful improvement for reteaching (Lewis & Tsuchida, 1997; Yoshida, 1999).

Students' thinking, learning processes, and strategies for solving problems are the focuses of the research lessons. As a result of carefully studying student learning and misperceptions of mathematics, members of the lesson study team begin exploring in a longitudinal way the relevant mathematical concepts related to the desired learning; thus promoting their own content understanding and developing shared professional knowledge. Table 1.A provides details for the lesson study process as it evolved in the Southwest.

Table 1.A   Brief Overview of the Lesson Study Process

The Lesson Study Process as Developed in the Southwest United States	
Step 1 *Identifying the problem and establishing the overarching goal*	We began with teachers and administrators looking critically at the mathematics curriculum in their schools, in relationship to what they know about their students' learning. This process involves looking at both what kids are having trouble learning and at how these concepts are currently being taught. We suggested: • *Engaging in a curriculum alignment process.* • *Developing an overarching goal for the school.* • *Thinking about and engaging in designing for understanding.* We also considered: • *What are the enduring understandings we want our students to have?* • *How will we assess students to know if they have these understandings?* • *What learning opportunities can be designed to support students' gaining this understanding?*
Step 2 *Developing the research question in the lesson study group*	We reflected on the overarching goal the team, school, or district developed for their students by asking: • *How can you relate this goal to the learning needs you identified in stage one?* • *Clearly identify the problem area you want to address. Then develop your question for the research you will be doing through lesson study.*
Step 3 *Designing the research lesson*	Once the student learning problem was identified, we addressed it here for planning. The research lesson must be developed in the context of the larger unit in which it exists and the overarching goal. A. We planned the context for the research lesson by considering: • *The mathematics or other content you want students to learn.* • *The communication and discourse you intend students to engage in.* • *The kinds of data you want to gather to answer your questions.* • *Considering principles related to engaged learning environments.* B. We used the research lesson format to plan the actual observation lesson. We spent time on each of the steps and put a special emphasis on what questions or problems students might have during the lesson. C. Prior to doing the lesson, share it with your mentor and other teachers via the Web and ask for ideas and feedback. Also, be clear about what data you want to gather and who will gather it.

(Continued)

Table 1.A (Continued)

The Lesson Study Process as Developed in the Southwest United States	
Step 4 *Doing and observing the lesson*	The research lesson gave us the opportunity to try out ideas in the real world of teaching practice. The time spent completing steps 1–3 helped us to realize our goals for student learning in the observed lesson. Two rounds of lessons are usually done, with an opportunity to revise between the lessons. We created observation guidelines and made sure that all observers had copies of the research lesson and understood what data they would be gathering. Every effort was made to not change the lesson dates. Teachers from other schools, preservice teachers, and staff provide valuable feedback, but would find it difficult to participate if the dates change.
Step 5 *Debriefing, reflecting on, and revising the lesson*	Immediately after the lesson, all those who observed the lesson spent an hour or so in a short debrief of the lesson. The debrief started by allowing first the teacher(s) who taught the lessons to comment on their reactions to what happened, followed by the team who designed the lesson. Then comments were encouraged from the outside observers, the teachers, and the staff. We also created debriefing guidelines. A second longer meeting was held a week or two later to further reflect on the lesson using the actual video record of the lesson and the data gathered by the observers. Completing two lesson cycles allowed us to continue with step 6, otherwise we would have repeated steps 1–3. One way we began this meeting was by looking back at the research question and then the process used in designing the lesson related to the question. **Design:** What was the planned learning for students? **Content:** What was the concept we wanted students to learn? What evidence did we have of their understanding or lack of understanding? **Discourse:** What discourse was planned and what kind of communication occurred? **Environment:** What did we learn about the learning environment? We hoped that the data gathered by the observers, as well as our own experiences in doing the lesson, would help answer these questions.
Step 6 *Sharing what we learned*	As teacher researchers we acquired valuable knowledge about how students learn and what kinds of instructional strategies seem to be most powerful for improving student learning. Just as sharing what they learned is an important part of student learning, sharing teacher research is a necessary final stage to each research lesson cycle. We had much to offer to the field and to our colleagues. We used the lesson study report guidelines.

The templates we used for design guidelines (steps 1–3), observation guidelines, debriefing guidelines, and final report guidelines are included in the additional support materials in Resource A.

The Role of Technology in Documentation and Lesson Study Practice

Because of grant funding, we were able to videotape many hours of lesson planning, teaching, debriefing, and reteaching. In fact, our first videographers, Kalle Jorgensen and Jennifer Villa, were trained in videotaping lesson study by Stigler's lesson lab team during the summer of 2002. We have extensive videotaped documentation, not only of the research lesson process, but also of our annual lesson study conferences, where groups of teachers presented their findings and submitted final reports on what they and their students learned from engaging in two cycles of lesson study each year. Reports, lessons, and teacher conversations regarding lesson study were also preserved electronically.

The use of technology makes possible the implementation of lesson study even across geographically diverse areas. New Mexico is a large state, and teachers doing lesson study in the MathStar project, which also occurred in Colorado and California, were often separated by many miles. We were fortunate to receive a grant from Hewlett-Packard that provided 100 laptop computers for teachers across the state who were engaged in lesson study. Teachers agreed to use the computers to communicate with each other about lesson study, to participate in two lesson study cycles, and to attend the annual lesson study conference to present their findings. Much of the lesson planning was done using Web chats and e-mail, in addition to the teachers driving to each other's schools for observing and debriefing research lessons. Teachers became adept at using computer programs to support their work, including using VideoCapture software to communicate what students were learning in their classrooms. Teachers also became adept at watching their videotaped lessons in preparation for the reteaching the lessons, a step we added to the lesson study cycle.

In the United States, there is a large range of experiences afforded through lesson study because of the different formats and levels of participation, the context in which it is implemented, and the role that lesson study is intended to play in professional development within a school or district. Thus, lesson study already has a different and more diverse history in the United States than in Japan. In Chapter 2 there are examples of different types of lesson study communities that have emerged in the United States. Further study is needed on the benefits and challenges of these diverse approaches. One of the key questions to be considered in looking at these implementation models is to what extent teachers choose to engage in lesson study. Some leaders in lesson study are adamant that teachers must choose to participate in lesson study for it to work. And yet, in some districts and schools, where those in charge of academic programs have chosen to institute lesson study or lesson modeling as the preferred methods of professional development, there have been positive responses from teachers and positive changes for students.

There has not been as much research on lesson study in the United States as we would like, partly because of its recent introduction in this country, and partly due to the lack of translated documentation in English of the process in Japan. However, this is changing. Fernandez and Yoshida (2004) have written a new book on Japanese lesson study that provides detailed guidance on the process through case studies in Japan and may be helpful to those desiring to implement it in the United States. Catherine Lewis, one of the early writers on lesson study in the U.S., first published what she had learned about Japanese educational practices in her book *Educating Hearts and Minds* (1995), years before *The Teaching Gap* (Stigler & Hiebert, 1999) was published. Lewis (2002) also published a clear explanation of the essential steps for doing this work in her book *Lesson Study: A Handbook of Teacher-Led Instructional Improvement*.

Notwithstanding the diversity of these efforts, a common theme emerges when teachers are asked about their lesson study experiences: teachers are taking increased ownership of their own work. Several months after the MathStar leaders made the change from a more traditional professional model to working with teachers on lesson study, the outside evaluator for the MathStar project (Wexford, Inc., 2003b) reported the following comment from one of the teachers about the changing focus of professional development:

> Originally it was to bring technology into the classroom. So at the beginning we received laptops, digital cameras, and printers, and MS [MathStar] showed us software to use in the classroom to enhance student learning. Last summer they introduced lesson study to us. So now the purpose of MS is to support collegial respect, sharing of best practices, sharing of expertise, and bringing all those parts together.

Initial Barriers to Lesson Study in the United States

In order to provide readers with a realistic picture of lesson study implementation in the United States, the following section addresses some of the initial barriers we experienced in introducing lesson study in our mathematics and science projects.

Teachers as Collaborative Designers

The first barrier uncovered was that the teachers in our project simply had no experience in working together to develop lessons. In addition, teachers in general did not see themselves as curriculum or instructional designers. Nor did they see their jobs as involving what they develop and study with other teachers. Their training usually involved implementing curricula developed by outside experts and available through their assigned textbooks. Teachers had very little experience working together in substantive ways. They expressed reluctance about sharing lessons, and held tightly to special lessons that they had developed through hard work on their own. They focused on lessons as individual endeavors.

Associating Observation With Evaluation

Teachers, even though they had agreed to participate in the collaborative lesson study process, were still uncomfortable at first in letting other teachers and observers into their classrooms. The initial debriefs of the lessons always started with comments from the teacher groups about how good the teacher who taught the lesson was—even if she or he wasn't—because teachers associated observations with evaluations and were concerned with pleasing each other.

At first, the teacher groups had a hard time seeing the initial lessons as something belonging to the group. The traditional process of teacher evaluation in most schools requires a principal to observe a lesson, not in terms of considering what students are learning, but for required annual evaluations of the teacher. In the United States, the cultural practice of an outsider entering a classroom was accompanied by feelings of being personally evaluated. It took nearly a year for teachers to accept the idea that outside observation was not about evaluating the teacher.

I remember at one lesson study debriefing how one teacher suddenly expressed the idea that this process [of lesson study] was much better than evaluation and if we could only do our evaluations this way everyone would benefit from the process, much more than from the current system. The group began to talk about how nice it would be to involve administrators in the process so that everyone could be learning. They asked if there was a way to work with the district to replace formal evaluations with the process of working together to improve lessons for students. Several of the teacher groups, after the first year, invited principals and administrators to join in the lesson observation and debriefing. This resulted in increased administrator support for lesson study. (Karin Wiburg, November 2003)

Deciding on the Research Lesson Topic

We discovered during the first year that teachers needed help in deciding what should be the content of their first lesson. Some had the mistaken idea that lesson study required them to make up a new lesson, rather than to think about changing how they were teaching an existing lesson. It was helpful to ask teachers to focus on concepts that the students were having trouble learning and to look at student test results for additional information about areas of weakness. From the beginning, even in our initial introduction of lesson study, we grounded the work by asking teachers to examine student work. Teacher teams were asked to do some informal classroom assessment of students in order to understand what their students understood. Evaluating these formative assessments together was an enlightening process, especially for high school teachers, who were sure that their students understood fractions until they asked them to explain what they knew about rational numbers. We explicitly encouraged teachers not to make up new lessons, but to use existing lessons and to focus on how they could teach those lessons in ways that would help more of their students to understand.

Lesson Study Versus Lesson Planning

Another problem encountered fairly early was that teachers were looking at the research lesson as a traditional lesson plan. This led us to develop templates that helped teachers to plan for the lesson in the context of school and unit goals for their students. We refined the research lesson template over time, so that at each step of the lesson teachers were asked to think about what might be common student misunderstandings and how they could plan to address these. These templates, which scaffolded the research lesson process, are included in the Resources for Chapter 1. We helped teachers to analyze how to gather data and which data would be most useful during a research lesson in order to answer their own questions.

Another basic problem seemed to be the use of the term "lesson study." Teachers at first thought the goal was to develop a perfect lesson. They fell back on their often unsatisfying work of being required to turn in daily or weekly lesson plans, and thus confused lesson study with lesson planning. Many teachers thought of lesson plans as lists of fun activities they would do with students. They often had in mind cool lessons that would engage students in interesting-looking activities, especially for those times when they were being observed or evaluated. In order to change this idea of lessons as activities, we introduced the backwards design process (Wiggins & McTighe, 1998) and helped teachers to reconceptualize lessons in terms of what they wanted students to understand, how they would assess this understanding, and finally, which procedures or activities they might use to lead the students toward understanding.

While the introduction of unit planning around student understanding helped somewhat in improving teachers' ideas of lessons, the real idea behind lesson study is not the lessons themselves, but rather how the lessons relate to student learning. In fact, at one point in our lesson study journey, one of us tried to rename what we were doing as *learning* study. It was thought that this new term might help teachers to focus on what students were learning or not learning, instead of worrying about how they were teaching.

The Culture of Teaching

Teachers were used to thinking of teaching as what they were telling students. We helped teachers develop an understanding of how they were working too hard at doing all the learning for their students. This was especially true when we worked with high school teachers. Together we watched videotapes of the lessons. The teachers soon recognized how anxious they were to answer students' questions quickly. It was as if they thought it was their job to make everything as easy as possible for the students, and never to let them struggle over the answer to a problem.

When students didn't seem to understand, the teachers would repeat the same things they had just said, maybe louder or slower, but usually in the same way. When we first introduced the idea of presenting students with a problem and letting them work in small groups to solve it, the teachers confessed to feelings that they weren't important if they weren't telling the students how to solve the problem. In videotaped sessions, teachers watched themselves moving too quickly to give students the right answers and began to recognize that perhaps they were working harder than the students.

Curriculum Alignment

One of the more successful experiences we had with lesson study was implementing it in a district that was using only one curriculum and text across all their schools. Everyone was integrating the same units at around the same time in this district, and it was in this district that lesson study worked especially well. Not only was the curriculum the same, but also the effort to improve mathematics teaching was supported at all levels, from the superintendent to the instructional assistants. In other districts, we found large differences within schools and between schools on what teachers thought they should teach about a subject. This made it difficult for them to work together to design a common lesson.

Lack of a Common Mathematics Curriculum

Another barrier we faced while implementing lesson study was that, unlike the situation in Japan, in the United States there is no common curriculum focused on the main concepts in mathematics to be taught at a specific grade level. Our teachers were asked to cover (and in their textbook-driven curriculum they felt they *had* to cover) many different kinds of topics over the course of a year, and as a result there was very little time to teach any of the topics in depth. Where a Japanese text might cover eight topics in a year, a middle school mathematics text in the U.S. might include more than 60 topics the teacher is expected to teach during the same period of time. How can teachers teach for deep understanding with so many topics?

In addition, the teachers often didn't understand enough mathematics content to teach in a manner that supports student-directed, problem-based learning. Without deeper math knowledge, teachers were uncomfortable allowing students to ask about alternative solutions or to construct new ways of solving problems. This eventually led us to an active alliance with mathematicians in our university, who are now working with us and with teachers on lesson study teams.

Classroom Discourse

We discovered that teachers needed support in developing and sustaining instructional discourse in their classrooms and in knowing how to ask questions that facilitate learning. Teachers knew how to present in front of the class and work individually with students, but they needed help in engaging students in whole-group discussions and problem solving. In addition, many teachers were not experienced in teaching for understanding or in designing lessons to facilitate understanding, as opposed to just giving students the correct procedures and answers.

A final challenge for developing mathematics discourse in the Southwest border areas was the large numbers of English Language Learners (ELLs) in our classrooms. This situation, and ways in which lesson study can help support ELLs and bilingual students, is discussed more fully in Chapter 2.

Toward Essential Elements and Principles of Lesson Study

Lesson study is becoming increasingly popular in the United States. Yet its popularity, like that of new ways of teaching or new curriculum, has made many lesson study leaders nervous, because—based on the history of U.S. educational reform—superficial implementation could lead eventually to lesson study becoming another failed educational fad. This is not uncommon in the United States when new learning approaches, such as whole language or new math, are introduced in ways that are detached from the deeper theoretical constructs that require understanding in order to make the approach effective. Superficial implementation often leads to pendulum swings, for example from whole language to phonics or from problem-solving approaches to back-to-basics. In fact, James Stigler, in the foreword to Fernandez and Yoshida's (2004) book on Japanese lesson study, comments:

> A superficial implantation of lesson study is not likely to have any positive impact on the learning of teachers and students, and given our impatient political climate, a lack of immediate results may well lead to lesson study being declared a failure before it is understood in any deep sense. (Fernandez & Yoshida, 2004, p. x)

At the 2003 annual conference of the American Educational Research Association (AERA), Catherine Lewis organized a meeting of key players involved in introducing lesson study across the U.S. She invited us all to reflect on and articulate what might be the essential elements or principles for practicing and researching lesson study. Deborah Ball, a well-respected mathematics educator, agreed to be the discussant for this presentation and provided feedback on what seemed to be common elements among all the efforts. A summary of promising principles is included below.

Common and Promising Elements of Lesson Study

1. Being instruction-centered and teacher-directed. Every presenter suggested centering reform in classrooms and under the control of teachers. Cohen and Hill (2001) write, ". . . challenging curricula have failed to impact on teaching and learning partly because teachers had few opportunities to learn and improve their practice" (p. 252). They also describe how efforts to reform teaching have failed because the professional development models used bore little resemblance to what teachers actually do with their students and how content is currently taught and assessed. If teachers are going to implement standards-based curricula and foster learning environments where inquiry, communication, and problem solving are key components, then a new, transformative professional development model must be adopted.

2. Scaffolding professional development. The lesson study process provides an organized system that helps teachers to investigate their students' learning. As the MathStar lesson study project evolved, we found ourselves designing and redesigning templates for setting goals, designing the research lessons, debriefing strategies, and gathering and reporting data. Our lesson study involved studying and refining our tools and presentations to increase learning for the teachers as they began to implement lesson study.

   Using video and technology tools helped us understand and scaffold our professional development in lesson study. We used these tools to develop video segments taken from teacher practice, exemplifying each stage of the lesson study cycle. Videotaping and video analysis also helped us to document and reflect on our work. The director for MathStar examined hours of video after the end of the first year of implementation and found several themes that emerged: teachers openly reflecting on their practice; an interest in what students understand and don't understand; an interest in student thinking; and a great deal of discussion about how to ask students questions rather than just tell them the answers.

Scaffolding is a very important and delicate process. Professional developers need to know how to provide structure without prescription. In many ways scaffolding is at the heart of successful teaching and can perhaps be most easily understood in terms of Vygotsky's notion of the *zone of proximal development* (Mooney, 2005). With teachers as well as students, it is important to ask what teachers can do with support and where they need to start, in order to avoid requiring teachers or students to complete tasks beyond their current levels of understanding. On the other hand, it makes no sense to teach something that has already been learned.

3. The potential of lesson study to help teachers learn academic content. There seems to be evidence that teachers can improve their understanding of content knowledge as a result of participating in lesson study. This was a common theme of the presentations at the AERA conference. Researchers have found that teachers' background and knowledge in the areas they teach makes a difference in student performance (Darling-Hammond & Sykes, 1999). Observations of teachers engaged in lesson study demonstrate the importance of teachers knowing the content in order to help the lesson flow. Deep content knowledge is also necessary in order for teachers to feel that they can explore students' questions and alternative answers to mathematics problems.

   As teachers watch lessons by those knowledgeable about content, they become interested in furthering their own backgrounds in an academic content area. In our own experience, after a year or two of lesson study, teachers began to want to understand deeply the content of mathematics they were teaching. During this time, we as facilitators asked the teachers to tell us: *Where is the math?* This became a familiar joke as we continued our lesson study journey. It also led us to invite content specialists to help us with lesson study work.

4. The need for redesigned time for professional development. Many of the successful lesson study programs involved grant funding, which provided release time or restructured days for

the teacher participants so that they had the time and space to engage in reflective practice. If schools and/or districts are serious about implementing this form of professional development, they must provide teachers with the necessary time. In Japan, such time is a component of the school day. School district partners in our newest mathematics grant have agreed to provide teachers with 1½ hours per week for collaborative mathematics study groups. Various options for finding time for lesson study are presented in Chapter 3.

5. Assistance from knowledgeable others. In all the presentations by experts from around the United States, the importance of mentoring by knowledgeable professionals was mentioned. In addition, expertise was necessary in areas related both to pedagogy and to content knowledge. The most successful models involve teams of education experts working with mathematicians—or other content experts—on lesson study teams. (In Japan, instructional supervisors are often involved in supporting lesson study at school sites.) Resources, electronic and print, also were deemed important. The use of videotaping and video analysis by the teachers was extremely important. Teachers in rural areas wanting to work on lesson study used interactive discussions via our Web site to further their work. Stigler has developed a Web-based Lesson Lab Program (see www.lessonlab.com) that provides scaffolding for teachers who are studying classroom events.

6. Well-aligned curricula and top-down and bottom-up support. In our work with lesson study teams, we found it easiest to work in districts that had a common mathematics curriculum, alignment of that curriculum with standards and assessment, and both top-down and bottom-up support for the curriculum, from the superintendent to the teacher in the classroom. Moreover, support from homes and communities for studying student learning and improving teaching has been helpful in facilitating lesson study. We are reminded of Robert Moses and his Algebra Project (see www.algebra.org), in which teachers, students, and parents worked together to understand algebra.

Chapter 3, on assessing your district's readiness for lesson study, will help you to decide if there are certain threshold conditions you should develop—such as a common curriculum or more time for teacher study—before undertaking lesson study. The alignment of the content area curriculum with district testing and teaching is also an important factor, although lesson study itself may be helpful in facilitating such alignment.

Conclusion

This chapter introduced the history of lesson study both in Japan and as it relates to educational issues and barriers to implementation in the United States. Barriers were presented, and essential elements common to a range of lesson study initiatives across the United States were introduced. Those interested in adopting lesson study in their schools and/or districts should consider the essential elements required for implementing lesson study.

Extended Learning Questions

1. Discuss the challenges to doing lesson study suggested by the authors in this chapter. Decide which of these barriers are likely to happen in your setting. Write or discuss how you might overcome these barriers.

2. Which part of the lesson study process might be exceptionally challenging for you to do? Talk about this.

3. Are there any differences between the Japanese and American educational systems that have not been mentioned in this chapter? Spend some time investigating these differences or those already mentioned. How important do you think these differences are in terms of successfully using lesson study in the United States?

2

Building Successful Lesson Study Communities

With David Rutledge and Rocio Benedicto

It takes a village to raise a child. It takes professional communities to make lesson study successful.

This chapter summarizes some of the common themes and elements that have emerged as lesson study has been implemented in diverse communities across the United States. In all cases, teachers experience similar challenges, as a fundamentally new kind of professional development comes up against a very familiar and basically traditional system of schooling. Neil Postman (1969) wrote a popular book in the 1970s—still frequently mentioned today—called *Teaching as a Subversive Activity*. What many people don't know is that several years later, as a result of what he had learned in trying to introduce change in schools, Postman (1979) wrote a book titled *Teaching as a Conserving Activity*. Like many who have researched the nature and organization of schooling in the United States, he concluded that the institution had been developed specifically to preserve and conserve our national values and way of life. This conservative model works well when new peoples—from many different cultures, languages, and social classes—need to be introduced to a relatively small data-base of knowledge and to fairly simple work opportunities upon graduation from middle or high school.

However, our world has changed dramatically and requires of students who graduate a variety of new kinds of learning abilities. Norton and Wiburg (2002) suggested that these new basic skills include: (1) literacy, not only of text but also of symbols, visual images, and so on; (2) problem-solving experience and skills; (3) knowledge of the structure and process of the disciplines; (4) information management and use; and (5) the ability to participate and work in diverse communities. These kinds of educational outcomes cannot be developed within a traditional system in which teachers are asked only to deliver information to students related to what we know from the past.

To graduate students capable of living and working in a rapidly changing world with a global economy, it is necessary to fundamentally change how teachers instruct and how students learn. We also know that change is difficult, because schooling itself exists as a strong culture built, in many ways, to be resistant to change. Changing a culture is slow and requires an approach to professional development that provides experiences in new kinds of cultural activities and settings. Whatever else is said about lesson study, it does provide a framework that supports cultural change in teaching. It accomplishes this by providing opportunities for teachers to examine and change their own practices in ways that will help students to become problem solvers, thinkers, users of information, and participants in diverse learning groups.

Toward Professional Development Communities

Professional development has evolved from one-shot, random workshops—or "drive-bys" as some PD providers call them—to sustainable forms that are intended to support ongoing changes in teaching and learning. We have come to see these changes in professional development as they relate to the culture of teaching. Lesson study, because it is based on the idea that teaching is a cultural activity, can provide the necessary structure that allows communities of teachers to study and make changes in the instruction they provide on a daily basis. Even when districts introduce the important notion of professional learning communities into their professional development plans, these communities need models, tools, and structures from which to work. Providing time for teachers to look at teaching together is only a beginning. Lesson study is a useful structure for making this time productive. It provides a well-defined process for sustainable professional development around what teachers are teaching and students are learning. One of the reasons that lesson study may be easier to introduce than some other educational reform agendas is that it is introduced in terms of lessons. Teachers already consider lessons to be a core cultural component of their work.

Lesson study is actually a form of action research, but in our previous work in conducting action research we found that it was difficult initially for many teachers to connect to the broad meaning of doing research. They had never seen themselves as researchers. However, by asking teachers to research the teaching of lessons to their students, which they see as central to their everyday work, the understanding of what it means to do research becomes more accessible.

Districts are often hesitant to introduce a form of professional development such as lesson study, which requires extensive teacher time and effort. However, if a school or district knows that the current instruction is not working for many students and wants to make fundamental changes in teaching and learning, time is required. It takes time to change cultural practices, and structuring that time so that teachers become leaders in the proposed changes through the lesson study process makes sense.

This chapter introduces a variety of different types of lesson study communities, beginning with the original MathStar project and expanding to describe newer lesson study communities that have emerged, including lesson modeling and whole-school lesson study models. It ends by describing in some detail how lesson study can help teachers of bilingual students to continue to move forward in content learning while understanding how language affects learning.

The Original MathStar Lesson Study Project

As noted previously, lesson study emerged in our region as a result of the frustration experienced by leaders in a mathematics professional development project: what teachers learned enthusiastically in summer institutes never seemed to make its way into the classroom. Prior to changing to lesson study, we had often asked teachers what they needed in their classrooms to help their students, but teachers were uncomfortable with answering such a vague and unfocused question.

The project had begun as a mathematics/technology project and had provided teachers with technology tools for mathematics, such as spreadsheet software and calculators. Sometimes the teachers used these tools as part of their instruction, but in general everyone kept on teaching in ways with which they were familiar, using the textbooks and materials provided by their districts. Once we began to use lesson study as the vehicle for improving teaching and learning, the teachers specifically commented on how much better the initiative was, because it considered their needs and the needs of their students. In 2003 our outside evaluators (Wexford, Inc., 2003) reported the following teacher comment:

> The original purpose was to help teachers integrate technology into curriculum. But they are listening to what we want and now it has evolved into a support base. Their purpose now is to give us tools to continue to support and improve ourselves. They are giving us the help to do the work ourselves after MS is gone, to improve our teaching, what we're teaching and what the kids are learning.

Another interesting finding concerned teachers' perceptions of themselves as members of a common professional community. At the beginning of the MathStar project, the rural teachers from very small schools and the more urban teachers had wondered how they could have anything to teach each other, since they worked in such different worlds. One of our schools had more cows than people and was almost 2 hours from the nearest city "large enough to have a Wal-Mart" (our teachers' words). As the teachers shared what they had learned during our second biannual lesson study meeting, they began to recognize that they all had comparable problems with teaching mathematics and that what they were doing to correct these problems was really quite similar. Their comments—in videos, in their reports, and in interviews with ourselves and our outside evaluators—reflected feelings of community. Issues of teaching and learning that emerged had deep underlying commonality across sites. Lesson study gave teachers the opportunity to investigate and discuss these learning problems together.

Toward the end of the first year, we looked at teachers' reports from their two rounds of lesson study, survey data about their experiences during the year, reports from the MathStar mentor teachers, and many hours of video of their lessons and debriefing sessions, and began to develop some initial frameworks related to what was happening.

Some teachers had explicit goals for researching student-centered teaching strategies. Others were starting to think about how to help students make connections, solve problems, collaborate, and communicate their reasoning both with their peers and by using the research lesson template materials themselves. Whenever we talked with teachers, we recognized that they were making great strides in meeting their goal of focusing on understanding their students' thinking. Teachers realized that they needed to know what their kids know. Many teachers said that, with every lesson they teach now, they think about what the kids need to know, what the students think, and how they can help them. In order to help them consolidate their learning, we asked teachers to reflect on what they had learned about instruction (in general and related to their research lesson), about student learning (in general and specific to their research lesson), and about the lesson study process.

The director for MathStar also looked at many hours of video and found several themes that emerged: Teachers openly reflecting on their practice; an interest in what students understand and don't understand; an interest in student thinking; and ideas about how to ask students questions rather than just tell them the answers.

The MathStar lesson study project was one of the first in the United States that was not at first initiated by teachers. This did not seem to be a detriment or limitation. Teachers embraced this new process, and because it was part of a grant-funded initiative they were provided with the time and support to engage in lesson study. Our teachers were given half a day of sub-time a month, and all teacher groups had facilitators who were themselves experienced school-based mathematics teachers. The facilitators were also assisted by university experts in pedagogy and mathematics. This facilitation, as well as the time provided to teachers, was key to the initial success of the project.

As the MathStar project grew to include more schools and teachers, with funding help from the districts and from the Hewlett-Packard Foundation, we were able to continue to provide teacher study time, facilitator support, and laptops for all the teachers. In addition to school-based research lessons, our teachers gathered twice a year to share their lessons with all the other teachers in the project. We soon recognized that this sharing was an essential part of lesson study.

The teachers in this diverse state project, who had initially huddled in their own regional groups, did not recognize what they had in common. After a year of implementing lesson study and our insisting that teachers present their lessons to each other and visit each other's sites to observe lessons, the diverse groups of MathStar teachers began to form a community. Thus, lesson study can help build community across diverse geographic regions and different kinds of schools. However, there was still a great deal of work to do to build a strong and sustainable lesson study community. After the first year, the director wrote a letter to teachers to support them in how far they had come and to suggest areas that still needed significant work.

This is a letter that is sent to the core teachers of the Lesson Study schools, the college of education of the universities, and the administrators of the school districts involved. The information in this letter gives the reader a broad overview of the expectations in expanding the Lesson Study Project to design the research around the lesson itself.

Lesson Study—A Continuous Improvement Process

Dear Core Teachers and University and School Collaborators,

Total quality management (TQM), quality circles, and lesson study are three reform movements that had their origins in the United States but actually came to fruition in Japan. All three are processes grounded in the notion of continuous improvements in practice, whether in business or education. We want to suggest in this letter what we might do to move to the next level of improvement in lesson study in our project.

Last year we worked on refining our research lesson design. This year we would like to work on designing the research around the lesson. Many of us recognized that we had not spent enough time seeing the research lesson as a window into the entire lesson study process. We need to spend more time on the research and reflection that surround the lesson, including:

- *The questions that are asked;*
- *The design of the unit from which the research lesson is drawn;*
- *The math content and discourse used;*
- *The kinds of data we want to gather to answer our research questions.*

At our summer institute we conceptualized some of our developmental needs in terms of more work in design, content, and discourse and in each of your groups there are people who are working on developing expertise in one of these areas. We also, with the help of Catherine Lewis, our summer consultant, worked on defining and refining the data we gather in connection to the research lesson.

Dr. Karin Wiburg,
Principal Investigator
for the Lesson Study Project

In order to help this work come to fruition we have designed a process that moves from identifying the learning problem you want to address, to designing the lesson, to gathering data to inform our decisions about further refining our work.

Here are some ideas you might try out as we begin to improve the process that surrounds the development of your research lesson.

Step 1—Identifying the Problem and Establishing the Overarching Goal

The lesson study process begins with teachers and administrators looking critically at their mathematics curriculum. Teachers need to examine the mathematics curriculum in their schools in relationship to what they know about their students' learning. Curriculum is not just material in books, but the interaction of students with the learning opportunities provided. This is a two-sided problem that involves looking at both what kids are having trouble learning and at how these concepts are currently being taught. We suggest:

A. Engaging in a curriculum alignment process

B. Developing an overarching goal for the school

C. Thinking about and engaging in designing for understanding

What are the enduring understandings we want our students to have?

How will we assess students to determine if they have these understandings?

What learning opportunities can be designed to support students' gaining this understanding?

Step 2—Developing the Research Question in the Lesson Study Group

Reflect back on the overarching goal that your team, school, or district has developed for your students. How can you relate this goal to the learning needs you identified in stage one?

Clearly identify the problem area you want to address. Then develop your question for the research you will be doing through lesson study. Here are some examples:

- *The problem area:* Students have a limited repertoire of learning strategies; teachers may not be teaching learning strategies like metacognition.
- *The question:* Will instruction in metacognition help students use more learning strategies?
- *Problem area:* Students don't seem to be able to visualize mathematics problems.
- *The question:* Will more work with visualization of mathematical relationships help students solve fraction problems?
- *Problem area:* Students are not critical about the data they generate using software applications.
- *The question:* How can we teach students to be critical users of technology-generated information and to test their results? What impact will this have on student learning?

Step 3—Designing the Research Lesson

Once you have identified the student learning problem you want to address, it is time for planning. The research lesson must be developed in the context of both the larger unit in which it exists and the overarching goal.

Plan the context for the research lesson by considering:

A. The mathematics or other content you want students to learn;

B. The communication and discourse you intend students to engage in;

C. The kinds of data you want to gather to answer your questions;

D. The principles related to engaged learning environments.

Use the research lesson format to plan the actual observation lesson. Spend time on each of the steps, and put a special emphasis on what questions or problems your students might have during the lesson.

Prior to doing the lesson, share it with your mentor and other teachers via the Web and ask for ideas and feedback. Also, be clear about what data you want to gather and who will gather it.

Step 4—Doing and Observing the Lesson

The research lesson is the opportunity to try out your ideas in the real world of teaching practice. The time spent completing steps 1–3 should help you to realize your goals for student learning in the observed lesson. Two rounds of lessons are usually done, with an opportunity to revise between the lessons.

Visit the observation guidelines and be sure that all observers have copies of the research lesson and understand what data they will be gathering.

Please make every effort to not change the lesson dates. Teachers from other schools, as well as preservice teachers, can provide valuable feedback but find it difficult to participate if the dates change. This is also true for the MathStar staff.

Step 5—Debriefing, Reflecting on, and Revising the Lesson

Immediately after the lesson, all those who observed the lesson should spend an hour or so in a short debrief of the lesson. The debrief should start by allowing first the teacher(s) who taught the lessons to comment on their reactions to what happened, followed by the team who designed the lesson. Then comments should be encouraged from the outside observers, the teachers, and the staff. See the debriefing guidelines. A second longer meeting should be held in a week or two to further reflect on the lesson using the actual video record of the lesson and the data gathered by the observers. If this is the first lesson cycle, go back to Step 2. If you have completed two lesson cycles, go to Step 6.

Step 6—Sharing What You've Learned

As teacher researchers, you have acquired valuable knowledge about how students learn and what kinds of instructional strategies seem to be most powerful for improving student learning. Just as sharing what they learned is an important part of student learning, sharing teacher research is a necessary final stage to each research lesson cycle. You have much to offer to the field and to your colleagues.

The original lesson study work occurred in teacher teams that were supported by a multistate mathematics initiative for middle school students. These teacher teams grew within New Mexico from 24 teachers to more than 100 teachers and eventually included groups of teachers in Colorado and California as well. This model involves teachers working on teaching and learning in a specific content area—in our case, mathematics.

The Emergence of Other Types of Lesson Study Communities

As the lesson study movement grows in the United States, it is emerging in a variety of forms. While these forms are different, many of them include support from university research and practitioners interested in improving students' learning. Some of the other forms of lesson study with which we are familiar include the following.

Lesson Modeling—A Way to Introduce Lesson Study

Sometimes schools are not ready to try a complete implementation of lesson study but would like to try a form of lesson study that doesn't require as much time and teacher effort as that demanded by a full implementation.

The Southwest Educational Development Lab (SEDL) in Texas developed an introductory approach to lesson study with a process that begins with lesson modeling. Lesson modeling is intended to introduce teachers to the process of planning and analyzing lessons in terms of their impact on student learning, and provides a way to introduce lesson study to new groups without requiring an extensive up-front commitment from districts or schools. It often invites instructional specialists from outside of the school to come into the classroom and model a lesson designed for increasing student understanding of a concept. Teachers can then discuss what they learned by watching this lesson, particularly what they learned about their lesson. A further explanation of lesson modeling can be found on the SEDL Web site www.sedl.org.

Teacher-Initiated Lesson Study Groups

A high school teacher from a rural area sent us an e-mail some years ago suggesting that he would like to write a better high school math curriculum for the Hispanic students he taught. We suggested he focus on classroom instruction, and on how the curriculum was taught, rather than developing another curriculum, many of which sit unused on teachers' shelves. We invited him to one of our early lesson study conferences. This teacher returned to his district and met with all the high school math teachers in the district, who decided that they wanted to form a lesson study team.

This model of lesson study included a strong teacher group—in fact, all the secondary-level mathematics teachers—which is still engaged in lesson study in spite of limited district administrative support and little funding for planning and release time. This second model is a teacher-driven lesson study model and in many ways is like the original lesson study teacher group that evolved in San Mateo, California under the leadership of Catherine Lewis from Mills College. We occasionally provided minimal support to this team, such as paying their expenses to attend annual lesson study conferences, but had little success in getting administrative support for teachers to receive sub-days or support for their work.

A Districtwide Professional Development Model

As a result of some contact with the original MathStar project, the mathematics curriculum director of a large urban district decided to introduce lesson study as the form of professional development for the district and used district funds to implement this process in all middle and elementary schools. When the professional development leader wanted to conduct lesson study, she invited teachers to attend a week-long conference sponsored by MathStar and facilitated by experienced lesson study teachers and experts such as Catherine Lewis, who had come from California to help us. At the end of the week most of the teachers had chosen to do lesson study. Those who didn't were not the focus of the district's professional development efforts.

This group consists of a large districtwide group made up of all K–8 mathematics teachers. The leader paid for teachers to attend an early one-week lesson study conference and then invited teachers to participate if they were interested. The teacher teams who indicated an interest were supported for the next 2 years by district professional development funds.

Whole-School Lesson Study Models

Another model that has emerged within the last 2 years is the use of lesson study as the form of professional development throughout the school. The leaders of the two schools in which this is occurring consider lesson study part of the catalyst they felt they needed for schoolwide reform. In the first case, lesson study became the sole form of professional development in a small, rural, dual-language (Spanish and English) elementary school.

Over the last 2 years Cathy Kinzer, who completed her dissertation on lesson study at this school, has been mentoring teachers in a dual-language school near the border with Mexico (Kinzer, 2005).

The principal had requested that lesson study be the only form of professional development to be used in her school for 2 years. What can be seen throughout the many hours of videotaping and interviews, the hours of classroom observations, and the recordings of biannual teacher presentations of findings is the growth of a professional development community. The principal had tried to get teachers to talk about their practice. In a videotaped interview at the beginning of the whole-school lesson study project, she said that she did not believe that the teachers would ever be able to share their professional practice. After 2 years of lesson study, the conversations teachers are having are fundamentally different, and they are anxious to share with their principal what they are learning about student thinking.

Lesson study has become the form of professional development for a second school, in the South Valley of Albuquerque, which is serving as one of the first schools within a new project called TODOS (or Teaching Mathematics to All). TODOS provides resources and support to schools that want to provide equitable and rich learning opportunities to all students, with an emphasis on Latino students.

Building Bilingual Lesson Study Communities

The 2000 U.S. Census estimated that by 2040, the Latino/Hispanic peoples of the United States will number approximately 25 percent of the total population. Presently, Hispanics make up 12 percent of the total population, or approximately 32.8 million people. One of the unique features of this book is the focus on how lesson study serves diverse students, many who have been at the bottom of the achievement gaps in mathematics and science in this country. Our first public lesson study in spring 2004 was held in a 98 percent Hispanic middle school located near the Mexican border. It is a 100 percent free lunch school, and the majority of students in the school are not native English speakers.

Work in linguistically diverse (especially Spanish-English) classrooms in the border area has been an integral part of our lesson study journey. We have found that lesson study has helped teachers in bilingual classrooms to develop eyes for their students' learning. Our middle school lesson study team from the Gadsden Border District was one of the most successful teams during the several years of the MathStar project. In fact, they were the first to present a public lesson. The students in the lesson were bilingual seventh-grade students learning mathematics. By listening in on some parts of this lesson, you can begin to see how this form of professional development can help others to understand some of the problems and opportunities of Spanish speakers who are learning mathematics.

This first public lesson study was an exciting time for the teachers of the Gadsden middle school team. They had been working with their students throughout the previous 2 years, learning how to engage them beyond the traditional teacher-student relationship. The team, made up of six teachers—five of whom had themselves been English Language Learners—had come to the process of lesson study motivated by the needs that they had observed in their students and their community. During the process of lesson study workshops, they had been able to engage in thinking beyond the traditional planning of lessons, which for this border team meant thinking about the different capital that their students bring into the classroom. The cultural capital included linguistic diversity, and for the first time the teachers had a space to think about the manner in which the language that their students were bringing into the classroom affected the understanding of the lessons that they were teaching.

The majority of the mathematics classrooms are called monolingual, and yet all the teachers in these classrooms admitted to using Spanish (the other language in this community) in their teaching when clarification of concepts was necessary before they were able to proceed with the lessons. The importance of understanding the mathematics concepts took precedence over any external assignment of language usage in the classroom. The consideration of what was most important for the students to understand was exclusively focused on the mathematics, with language serving the utilitarian purpose of being the tool through which the concept or understanding could be internalized. The fact that this team of teachers chose the only ESL-designated classroom as the one that would be showcased in the public lesson highlights the manner in which this group of educators viewed the importance of language in the ability to mediate understanding in the mathematics classroom.

When a student doesn't understand certain mathematics concepts and can seek assistance from a bilingual mathematics teacher, the opportunity for learning is much greater because of the educator's preparation, not only in mathematics but also in addressing the needs of linguistically diverse students. Understanding the concepts becomes more important than the language of exchange. This was best exemplified when, in the course of the public lesson, the students—who were anxious both for themselves at being put on public display and for their teacher, with whom they had good rapport—had been trying to discuss the math problem at hand (having to do with scale) in English, a language with which most of them were not comfortable. Upon recognizing that this effort was impeding the manner in which the students were processing the problem, the lead teacher announced to the students that they should not be afraid to speak in Spanish, that it was okay, and that everyone understood it. This could only be done because of the lesson study process and the agreement by the team of teachers that what was most important in the mathematics classroom was the understanding of the concepts and not the language that was used to understand those concepts. This was also seen in the public lesson, when one of the teacher observers recognized that the pair she was observing had translated the concept of scale as "volume" and were trying to solve the problem with formulas for volume. It was during the debriefing that the teachers began to discuss why that particular pair had strayed so far from the correct answer. The lesson study team had predicted several scenarios that other teams had reported, but this scenario had not been foreseen.

The teacher observer said that the students had understood the problem as it was stated. They had written it down and had worked with the materials that had been provided in an appropriate manner. In other words, their behavior made it obvious that they had understood the teacher's instructions. So what happened? Where other teams had come up with reasonable ratios, this team had come to a conclusion that was four to five times the ratio of the other answers. The students had all taken their work with them, so it could not be seen by the debriefing team (the students had to continue to work on the assignment), but speculation continued about why that particular pair had understood so differently. Language was finally brought up as a topic, and suddenly it was as if a veil had been lifted, and a dawning awareness struck the group as they concluded that somehow scale had turned into volume in these students' mental processes. The question was: How did that happen? The lesson presentation script was reviewed. The language used was dissected, and the teachers dicovered that during the presentation the words that had been used were: "How can you fill this page up . . .?" The words "fill up" became the point at which this particular pair had understood "finding scale" as "finding volume." In Spanish, *llenar* (fill) is related to volume. This pair, who were being asked to find the best way to "fill" the grid paper that they had been given, thought were being asked to find the *volume* of something, which led them to the larger numbers, which they concluded would best find their solution.

The power of the lesson study process for bilingual educators, in mathematics or any other content area, lies in the ability to have the kind of exchanges in which they are able to decide and contextualize the understandings that their students are making in their classrooms. The process of coming together as a community of learners with specific expertise encourages professional engagement and empowers bilingual teachers to think about their practice and their students.

Lesson Study and Content Learning: The Mathematically Connected Communities Project

One of the weaknesses we found in early implementation of lesson study was that teachers often lacked the depth of understanding in the content area that would enable them to comfortably introduce problems in their classes and be able to provide structured help to students in how to solve those problems. The latest chapter in our story is an emerging community of lesson study practice that includes interactions between ourselves as educators and a group of seven university mathematicians, who began working with us and the teachers in the spring of 2004. At a recent meeting of the State Mathematics and Science Partners Group, one of the mathematicians spoke about how much he valued the opportunity, language, and tools provided by educators, because these gave him a way to look at his own teaching practice. While our journey with the math department began with our need as educators to have mathematicians help us and our teachers acquire increased mathematics content knowledge, the result has been an emerging form of lesson study, in which mathematicians are looking at their own teaching practice in the university.

As the lesson study community grew in the schools, teachers recognized a need for help from mathematicians, and a group of interested mathematics professors from the university were invited to join in several lesson study groups. These professors began to take a leadership role in supporting lesson study at both the high school and middle school levels. Their mathematics department received a grant from the Mathematics Institute of Park City, Utah to develop two new high school groups during the 2004–2005 school year. Lesson study was integrated into the fieldwork required by our university preservice mathematics methods classes and by a technology integration preservice class. Lesson study was also integrated into a science teacher initiative at the fourth- to eighth-grade levels.

An additional component of our partnership between educators and mathematicians is the development of a Master of Arts in Teaching Mathematics, as well as the development and offering of 2 years of summer academies, which focus on the learning of mathematics for teaching mathematics. Both these academies include lesson study, in which attending teachers instruct groups of middle school students on campus in one of the new mathematics concepts the teachers have been learning.

Integrating Lesson Study With Other Initiatives

In addition to integrating lesson study into new grant initiatives developed through the New Mexico Learning Collaborative, we have also used lesson study as a means for strengthening other, existing school initiatives. This is discussed more fully in Chapter 7. One example describes how lesson study was used to increase the positive impact of teachers learning to integrate technology in their classrooms by forming lesson study groups specific to their schools.

Conclusion

Chapter 2 has provided information on the variety of different forms of lesson study that emerged naturally during the implementation of lesson study in United States. These communities include teachers working together across states or distant rural communities, often within a grant-funded project. Some school districts have adopted lesson study as their form of professional development in a specific content area. Two schools have adopted a whole-school lesson study model as their form of professional development. In this model, and also in the Technology for Improved Achievement Regional Educational Technology Assistance Program (TIA RETA) model, lessons were done across different subject areas. No matter what form of lesson study we observed, the same key themes emerged. Teachers were empowered to see themselves as developers and assessors of lessons; there was an increased focus on student learning; and teachers began to design classroom activities in which they encouraged student dialogue and presentations.

Extended Learning Questions

---

1. Examine your own organization in which you hope to do lesson study. Identify the types of expertise that are present in your group. Are there people who can be content leaders and pedagogy and curriculum experts, as well as people skilled in facilitation of group processes? Begin to design an organization that includes the appropriate knowledgeable others. Your plan might begin with a graphic design for your lesson study community.

2. As teachers reflect on what research they would like to do in relation to teaching and learning, identify the kinds of experts who could help you with this research. Contact several experts and ask them for assistance with your lesson study research.

3. Become familiar with the notion of pedagogical content knowledge— Shulman (1987) is known for beginning this work—in the content area in which you will be doing lesson study. Research other sites where teachers have worked on pedagogical content. Approach experts in your district or nearby higher education institutions who have content knowledge, and ask them if they are interested in how to teach the content. Invite content experts to visit your school and classroom.

4. If you plan to do lesson study on mathematics teaching and learning, contact the Center for Teaching Mathematics at the University of Michigan and find out about their Survey for Content Knowledge in Mathematics Teaching Assessment Tool. This survey, which has been developed over many years, is a powerful means of assessing the effect of professional development on teachers' pedagogical content knowledge.

5. Begin to write a guidebook for organizations interested in doing lesson study. Include suggestions on how to develop the required expertise needed to successfully engage in lesson study.

3

Assessing Your Readiness for Lesson Study

Educational leaders must create artful ways to reweave organizational tapestries from old traditions, current realities, and future vision. This work cannot be done by clinging to old ways, emulating principles from effective schools and excellent companies, or divining futuristic images from what we imagine the next decade will be like. Rather, it takes a collective look backward, inward, and ahead.

—Terrence E. Deal (1990)

Lesson study, to be successful, requires the presence of a number of threshold conditions. These include curriculum alignment, including an alignment of curriculum, standards, teaching, and assessment; agreement on curricular goals and processes across the school and preferably the district; readiness to support new forms of professional development; and the ability of teachers to define student learning goals. Some organizations are at the point, for whatever reason, that they have decided that more of the same is not what they want. This chapter provides several tools for assessing your readiness to change, and shares findings from the leaders of successful lesson study projects about how and when to adopt a lesson study approach to improve student learning.

All these factors will be discussed in this chapter, but first we'd like to set the stage by discussing the emergence of new forms of professional development, including a reference to the recommendations of the National Staff Development Council (NSDC) and how these fit with adapting lesson study within your organization.

For too many years, conventional professional development for teachers has consisted of a smorgasbord of adult learning activities with few measurable results other than the continuation of a trend in which many teachers leave the profession within 5 years (National Center for Education Statistics, 1999b). In fact, many of the teachers who leave are the most creative and talented teachers, and the kinds of teachers who would be of great assistance in redesigning classroom instruction. Perhaps being the recipients of what have been called "teacher proof materials"—as well as being faced with often changing dictates from the administration about exactly how to improve achievement—might contribute to some of the brightest and most creative teachers moving on to another profession. We believe that lesson study can reverse the common top-down form of professional development and provide an environment for teacher-driven practice that could encourage many teachers to become research-based practitioners and stay in the schools.

Assessing Your Readiness for New Forms of Professional Development

Looking at professional development historically, little has changed. During a recent focus group, a member of our learning collaborative observed that if Rip Van Winkle woke up today, he would recognize two things—churches and schools. Many classrooms look like the classrooms of the 1950s: Teachers are still standing in front of the classroom talking; students are reading the textbook and answering questions; vocabulary lists are being memorized; and students are completing thousands of math problems with little or no understanding.

But as mentioned in Chapter 1, the world has changed a great deal, and so have the students we teach. While our classrooms become increasingly diverse in terms of ethnicity and language, teachers get little help in learning to meet the needs of these different students in their classrooms across the nation (Kardos, Johnson, Peske, Kauffman, & Liu, 2001).

Recent research into how teachers feel about current professional development efforts reinforces that there is a mismatch between what teachers need and what they are given:

- Only 18 percent of U.S. teachers rated their professional development experiences as "highly useful" in a 2000 survey (Schools and Staffing Survey, 2000).
- Only 48 percent of U.S. teachers reported more than 9 hours of in-depth professional development content during 2003 (Ingersoll, 2003).
- A large percentage—46.2 percent—of new teachers leave teaching within the first 5 years (NCES, 1999b).
- There is a 16 percent turnover per year for math and science teachers (Schools and Staffing Survey, 2000).
- 45.9 percent of math and science teachers cite poor administrative support as their reason for leaving teaching (Schools and Staffing Survey, 2000).

In short, reconceptualizing teaching as a cultural activity is an important initial step in order to reverse the trends indicated by these reported statistics. In order to create change in classroom learning, we must change the culture of teaching, not simply provide more activities, more workshops, or another list of recommendations (Hiebert & Stigler, 2004). Changing the culture of teaching is difficult, because it is integrated with the culture of education. Education is the one profession in which everyone was exposed to models of teaching as they grew up. We all attended school, and because of that experience a large segment of the public believes it has the right answers to our educational problems. We have heard politicians say: "If it was good enough for me, then it is good enough for our children." Many teachers were successful students and often served in roles of helping the teacher as they grew up. These teaching strategies worked for them during the period when they were successful students.

The problem, as mentioned earlier, is that our society and our clients have changed in fundamental ways. The student outputs of schools that worked in a simpler industrial age have become dysfunctional in an age when students need to learn how to think for themselves, work together with diverse groups, and comprehend and solve complex problems. In addition, the demographics of our students have changed. Our story of implementing lesson study in the United States is particularly relevant, since the Southwest border states are a microcosm of the future of all classrooms in the United States. Professional development models that work to improve teacher and student learning in diverse settings are of particular promise in improving teaching and learning across the country in the future. One member of our learning group likes to say: "Remember, we are the lab for the country."

The Beginning of Our Lesson Study Journey

As mentioned earlier, we chose to begin using lesson study because traditional models of professional development were not working in terms of changing what was happening in classrooms and/or improving student achievement. We had offered traditional summer workshops, in which we planned all the activities for the teachers. When we followed up by observing classrooms in the following months, very little of what the teachers had learned and practiced in the workshops seemed to have found its way into their classrooms.

A large study in St. Louis, Missouri, noted that, a year into a reform initiative, two-thirds of the 715 teachers who had received professional development had fallen back on traditional strategies despite the "reform initiative training." Two years later only teachers in a few schools seemed to be working toward the goal of full new-model implementation, with no schools making an effort for provide comprehensive staff support (Kedro, 2004).

We needed a model for professional development that promoted student learning while also empowering the teachers. A basis for reforming professional development is to follow the national guidelines from the NSDC.

National Staff Development Council's Recommendations

The NSDC provides the following guidelines:

- The goal of professional development is increased student learning.
- To achieve high levels of student learning, teachers must develop new knowledge, skills, attitudes, and behaviors.
- Professional development must be planned, designed, and implemented in ways that increase educators' capacity to impact students' learning, and the organizational structures, policies, and practices must be aligned to support the professional development program and goals (Roy & Hord, 2004).

We accepted these goals, along with the research that suggested the importance of the teacher. The teacher is the most important factor impacting student learning (Jordan, Mendro, & Weerasinghe, 1997; Rivkin, Hanushek, & Kain, 2002). Quality teaching matters even more than the socioeconomic level of the students (Darling-Hammond & Sykes, 1999). We needed a model that put teachers' beliefs and teachers' changes in practice at the center. And we needed to find a way for teachers to have time to talk and work together.

J. Killion (2002) provides a slightly different and broader assessment of how education and evaluation are now emerging in schools. We believe that this table is an excellent overview of the changes involved in moving from top-down and centralized professional development to newer forms that provide options for teachers as professionals to contribute to solving the teaching and learning problems in schools.

The practice of lesson study reflects many of the changes suggested by research.

Changing the Approach to Professional Development (Killion, 2002)	
FROM	**TO**
Externally driven and designed	Internally driven and designed
Summative evaluations only	Planning formative and summative evaluations
Event-based	Program-based
Looking for answers and solutions from others	Discovering or creating solutions and alternatives with others
Feared	Embraced
Filed/shelved	Used
Done as an afterthought	Planned from the beginning
Documentation	Evaluation
Process-focused	Results-focused
Presentation of results	Reflective dialogue

Lesson Study and the NSDC Recommendations

Research on best practices, as well as the recommendations of the National Staff Development Council, are discussed in the following section in terms of how a lesson study professional development program fits with these recommendations. The goal of lesson study is for teachers to work together to design learning opportunities or lessons that help more of their students to learn and to learn at a deeper level. This goal brings together the two essential desired outcomes of meaningful professional development, teacher learning and student learning.

As lesson study practitioners, we are aligned with the NSDC recommendation that, in order to increase student achievement, the change needs to be driven by teachers and involves nothing less than teachers developing new knowledge, skills, attitudes, and behaviors. One might even argue that it involves nothing less than changing the culture of teaching.

Over the last 20 years we have found teacher action research to be an effective process for sustainable improvements in teaching and learning, though it seems at first to be a very slow process. In fact, slow may not necessarily be bad. Piaget once commented that American educators are always interested in how fast students can learn and how they can speed up the process. Yet, experienced educators recognize that our system often embraces rapidly changing solutions for schools that swing back and forth like a pendulum, for example from whole language to phonics, and from mathematical computation to problem solving. The problem is that all these ideas for improvement are often separated from the theoretical frameworks from which they were developed. They are understood and implemented at a very superficial level. In fact, a former superintendent and friend has suggested that educators are fond of planting trees and then pulling them up before they have had a chance to take root. If lesson study is to have a positive effect on teachers and students, it must not be seen as another magic bullet. The principles behind lesson study, discussed further in this chapter, must be understood. But first let us suggest the following steps to our readers interesting in using lesson study:

1. Assess the readiness of your organization to change;

2. Consider the alignment and quality of your curriculum;

3. Think about the principles from which lesson study has emerged; and

Lesson Study and the NSDC Recommendations

Research on best practices, as well as the recommendations of the National Staff Development Council, are discussed in the following section in terms of how a lesson study professional development program fits with these recommendations. The goal of lesson study is for teachers to work together to design learning opportunities or lessons that help more of their students to learn and to learn at a deeper level. This goal brings together the two essential desired outcomes of meaningful professional development, teacher learning and student learning.

As lesson study practitioners, we are aligned with the NSDC recommendation that, in order to increase student achievement, the change needs to be driven by teachers and involves nothing less than teachers developing new knowledge, skills, attitudes, and behaviors. One might even argue that it involves nothing less than changing the culture of teaching.

Over the last 20 years we have found teacher action research to be an effective process for sustainable improvements in teaching and learning, though it seems at first to be a very slow process. In fact, slow may not necessarily be bad. Piaget once commented that American educators are always interested in how fast students can learn and how they can speed up the process. Yet, experienced educators recognize that our system often embraces rapidly changing solutions for schools that swing back and forth like a pendulum, for example from whole language to phonics, and from mathematical computation to problem solving. The problem is that all these ideas for improvement are often separated from the theoretical frameworks from which they were developed. They are understood and implemented at a very superficial level. In fact, a former superintendent and friend has suggested that educators are fond of planting trees and then pulling them up before they have had a chance to take root. If lesson study is to have a positive effect on teachers and students, it must not be seen as another magic bullet. The principles behind lesson study, discussed further in this chapter, must be understood. But first let us suggest the following steps to our readers interesting in using lesson study:

1. Assess the readiness of your organization to change;

2. Consider the alignment and quality of your curriculum;

3. Think about the principles from which lesson study has emerged; and

4. Consider whether your district and/or school and your teachers are ready to create the necessary conditions that will allow teachers to collaborate for change.

Assessing Your Organization's Ability to Change

One of the authors was involved in implementing the federally funded Preparing Teachers to Teach with Technology (PT3) grant some years ago and participated in a national evaluation effort led by Wexford, Inc. to investigate factors that seemed to be present in successful professional development programs (see www.wexford .org). It turned out that one of the critical factors for success in implementing a PT3 project was simply readiness for change. We believe that readiness for change is also a critical factor in whether a school district is ready to do lesson study. We recommend that you check out the entire Wexford Web site at www.wexford.org and the variety of tools available not only to assess change capacity, but also to learn more about leadership, teaching, and learning factors. We have received permission from Wexford to include in this book two Wexford Planning and Review Tools: Creating Organizational Change (Wexford, 2003a) and Indicators of Sustained Change (Wexford, 2003c). The surveys are included below and should be helpful in deciding whether your organization is ready for change and has some knowledge of how to guide and sustain change. The tools were developed with the help of national experts and include an assessment of the current organizational climate and culture. These questions are highly relevant to adopting a lesson study approach to professional development. You are welcome to adapt them to your own organizational needs, however, you must request permission to Wexford, Inc. in using these tools. See the Change Tools on the next three pages.

Assessing the Alignment and Quality of the Curriculum

One of the reasons that lesson study is so successful in Japan is that there is a very tight curriculum guide for teaching content. The guide also provides extensive information on how students learn concepts developmentally, and thus provides direction on when it is best to teach which concepts. Teachers are deeply familiar with the content and its sequence, and this content is similar from school to school.

(Text continues on page 47)

CREATING ORGANIZATIONAL CHANGE TOOL

Rating Scale   0: No   1: A little   2: Somewhat   3: A lot

Creating Organizational Change **A: Elements of Current Organizational Climate and Culture**				
1. There is dissatisfaction with the status quo related to the area of proposed change.	0	1	2	3
Comments:				
2. The organization supports the development of knowledge and skills for the people who will be called upon to do the new work in a changed environment.	0	1	2	3
Comments:				
3. The organization provides easy access to the resources needed to make the innovation or change work.	0	1	2	3
Comments:				
4. The organization supports the people who will be implementing the change by providing them with time to learn, adapt, integrate, and reflect on what they are doing.	0	1	2	3
Comments:				
5. There are rewards or incentives for participants.	0	1	2	3
Comments:				
6. There is evident organizational leadership.	0	1	2	3
Comments:				
7. There is unqualified and enthusiastic commitment to the change by the administration.	0	1	2	3
Comments:				
8. Participation in the change effort is expected and encouraged by leaders in the organization.	0	1	2	3
Comments:				

Creating Organizational Change B: "Fit" of Proposed Change into Current Organization				
1. The proposed change is better than what is there now.	0	1	2	3
Comments:				
2. The proposed change is the best alternative for addressing an unmet need.	0	1	2	3
Comments:				
3. The organization is able to support this change, either in whole or in stages.	0	1	2	3
Comments:				
4. The complexity of the innovation or change is compatible with what is currently done in the setting.	0	1	2	3
Comments:				
5. People can observe the innovation or change being used by others before deciding whether to adopt it.	0	1	2	3
Comments:				
6. People in the organization are already familiar with using technologies.	0	1	2	3
Comments:				
7. The organization is already using innovative and/ or learner-centered teaching and learning approaches.	0	1	2	3
Comments:				
8. People in the organization have established working relationships with colleagues in other organizations who are using similar innovations for similar purposes.	0	1	2	3
Comments:				

SOURCE: Forms from the www.wexford.org, Aug., 2004 Web site; used with permission.

INDICATORS OF SUSTAINED CHANGE TOOL

Rating Scale   0: No   1: A little   2: Somewhat   3: A lot

Indicators of Sustained Change **Elements of Institutionalization of the Innovation or Change**				
1. The innovation or change has been accepted by relevant participants and stakeholders.	0	1	2	3
Comments:				
2. The use of the innovation is stable and used routinely.	0	1	2	3
Comments:				
3. The innovation or change is used throughout the institution or organization.	0	1	2	3
Comments:				
4. People expect that the use of the practice or innovation will continue within the organization.	0	1	2	3
Comments:				
5. Continuation depends on the organizational culture, structure, or procedures rather than the actions of specific people.	0	1	2	3
Comments:				
6. Organizational time and money are routinely allocated to maintain and continue the change.	0	1	2	3
Comments:				

SOURCE: Forms from the wexford.org Web site, August, 2004; used with permission.

In the United States, a movement emerged in the 1960s to develop standards to ensure that what was taught in any part of the country was also taught in others. For many teachers, standards become confused with the whole idea of standardization, as well as standardized testing. In fact, standards are about determining which key ideas are to be taught in each subject area at each grade level. We do not recommend that teachers design the content of lessons. Instead, teachers should be using a standards-based curriculum and then design the teaching of the content together. We have a series of activities in which we engage teachers before beginning work with lesson study. Without a coherent curriculum in which learning outcomes for students are clear, it may be difficult to do lesson study.

In their book *Learning Policy,* Cohen and Hill (2001) argue for alignment in educational efforts, from state policy to teacher decisions in the classroom, and suggest that past educational reforms have failed because they failed to involve the teacher. The key to successful educational reform is working as closely as possible with teachers, with the curriculum they are supposed to teach and with the students they serve. This is one of the principal messages of this book, which you will hear in various forms throughout the chapters.

Activities for the Analysis of the School's Data

First, the teachers must know what their state is mandating for them to teach in their classrooms. For example, we are using our own state's standards in the field of mathematics, but of course readers can easily duplicate these activities using their own state's standards and any content field that contains national standards. The process of the activity would be the same.

The activities for assessing the alignment of the curriculum were initially developed from 1999 to 2004 as part of MathStar, a federally funded math grant. These activities are appropriate for you to use in working with teachers to align your school or district curriculum. The table on the next page shows a possible format for introducing the standards to teachers. Additional activities are included in the Resources in this book.

The Importance of Process Standards

We have found in our work that it is the process standards (reasoning, representation, problem solving, and so on) that are especially relevant to students doing well on assessments and

Activity 1 Understanding Standards	
Purpose	To familiarize participants with the state standards and benchmarks, including both process and content standards. The process standards describe the ways in which content should be taught, to facilitate the understanding that students should gain from their classroom experience. The content standards are a list of grade-level benchmarks and performance indicators that detail the specific content areas that students are expected to develop at each grade level.
Materials Needed	• PowerPoint presentation. • Copies of your state's math standards, including both content and process standards.
Estimated Activity Time	20 minutes
Steps for Facilitation	1. Introduce presenters and welcome participants. Quickly survey participants by finding out who is in the audience (grade levels of teachers, administrators, and so on). You may want to ask what experience the group has with the new math standards. 2. Walk the group through the PowerPoint presentation, stopping for questions when necessary. When discussing the content standards, let participants know that they will be selecting one content standard to focus on for Activity 3.

standards-based tests. We are fortunate that both process and content standards are aligned with our state standardized tests for grades 3–11. If your testing is not aligned with your standards, the problem of aligning the curriculum is more complex, and a careful analysis of what is on the test and how it relates to the standards is necessary. Please see Activity 3, Understanding Process Standards, in the additional support materials in Resource B.

Data Collection and Analysis

Data collection and analysis are integrated throughout this book, and often ground all reform efforts in schools. It is necessary to know how and what the students are learning based on standardized and informal test results, as well as informal preassessments, which are often used as an initial part of planning for lesson study.

This is the age of accountability as led by the federal mandate of No Child Left Behind. There are scores galore, including Terra Novas, Iowas, CATs, SATs, Accelerated Reader test results, graduation rates, grade point averages, state assessments, and more! Whether a teacher or administrator agrees or disagrees with all the testing, the data are there and can be used for good professional development that relates to increased student achievement. Too often, teachers do not understand the data and think of data only in a punitive fashion, as something by which they are judged. It is time to change this perception and help teachers to use the data to close the gap between school or district learning goals and actual student performance. As Repetti stated, it is wonderful when there is ". . . an 'aha!' moment that helps forge bonds that lead to teamwork, a literacy initiative, and higher scores" (Repetti, 2004, p. 138). There are programs, such as the NSF Using Data Project, that help educators develop data literacy:

> The ability to examine multiple measures and multiple levels of data to consider the research, and to draw sound inferences. Teachers and administrators become data facilitators, leading school data teams to dig deeply into several data sources, and through reflective dialogue, learn to improve mathematics and science teaching and learning. (Love, 2002, p. 97)

Data analysis is a very important step in determining the readiness of a school and its teachers for lesson study. Teachers must understand where their students are in the learning process; where the gaps are between the state standards or benchmarks and classroom teaching; and where the gaps in learning are between what students understand and what is asked on the state standardized tests. Teachers become the change agents within their own schools when they are given the lens to analyze the data and the voice for determining strategies to impact the learning of their students. Becoming change agents is very empowering and will lead teachers to use data as a lever for change, as documented in Nancy Love's

(2002) book, *Using Data/Getting Results: A Practical Guide for School Improvement in Mathematics and Science.* These ten ways include:

1. Uncover problems that might otherwise remain invisible.

2. Convince people of the need for change.

3. Confirm or discredit assumptions about students and school practices.

4. Get to the root causes of problems.

5. Help schools evaluate program effectiveness and keep the focus on student learning results.

6. Provide the feedback teachers and administrators need to keep going and stay on course.

7. Prevent an overreliance on standardized test scores.

8. Prevent one-size-fits-all and quick-fix solutions.

9. Give schools the ability to respond to accountability questions.

10. Help build a culture of inquiry and continuous improvement.

Included in the Resources is an activity for helping teachers to map the standards against what they are currently teaching, as well as suggestions for looking at how deeply and how frequently the standards are taught. Teachers are asked to examine their own standards and then mark them according to a color-coding process. For example, in one of these exercises, teachers would mark a standard as green when it is substantially covered in their classroom, yellow if it is partially covered, and pink if this standard is not currently taught, or is covered only in an extremely brief way. We have found this exercise to be extremely effective in helping teachers see for themselves how their teaching aligns with standards.

Curriculum Mapping

Curriculum mapping is similar to lesson study in that it facilitates teachers working together to solve problems in relationship to their practice. Like lesson study and action research, it solves the problem of teachers being separated from key decisions related to curriculum and teaching. The focus is on the curriculum. Working together, teachers understand what they are teaching and how it relates to larger school goals, standards, and the assessments used in their school or district.

Curriculum mapping is one way to address the curriculum alignment issue. Teachers develop personal maps of what they are teaching, organized by months over the school year, and then compare their maps to understand what concepts are being taught at which grade levels and in which subjects. Like lesson study, the ultimate goal of curriculum mapping is to increase learning opportunities for students and eventually to improve student achievement. In his most recent book, *Getting Results With Curriculum Mapping,* Jacobs (2004) defines curriculum mapping as "a procedure for collecting data about the operational curriculum in a school or district and referencing it directly to the calendar" (p. 1). He also helps administrators to consider how to introduce curriculum mapping and connect the process to an analysis of student learning needs.

As with lesson study, curriculum mapping requires leaders and knowledgeable others to introduce and facilitate the process. Leaders need to provide time for teachers to work together and ensure that the work is aligned with student learning needs and school goals. This process is similar to some of the workshop ideas we've suggested for understanding standards and then connecting them with teaching and with student learning needs. Leaders such as principals, curriculum directors, and/or master teachers must provide a clear process, including checklists and other guiding forms to ensure that teacher groups follow a defined process.

Again, like lesson study, curriculum mapping begins with what kinds of students teachers would like to see their students become. Jacobs (2004) reports a goal in one school as, "increasing our students' willingness to take risks when writing and to treat peers with more respect" (p. 2), which seems remarkably similar to the overarching goal suggested at the beginning of the lesson study process.

While we prefer ultimately that teachers engage in a process of teaching, observing a lesson, and reflecting together as well as planning, curriculum mapping is a model that helps teachers to understand and align their professional work with each other and with school goals, standards, and district assessments. Such planning and alignment of the curriculum may be important initial steps before teachers begin to develop units and, ultimately, research lessons. Unlike Japan—where the curriculum already is deep and tight and the same across all schools—a common understanding of what students need to know and be able to do at each grade level is a key prerequisite to being able to implement lesson study successfully in the United States. Here is an example of one professional development exercise used to help teachers map the curriculum.

In an earlier activity, teachers identified the gaps in their curriculum by comparing what is being taught to the standards. In this activity, teachers look at the data to see how these gaps are affecting student achievement. Later, teachers will use this knowledge to

Professional Development Activity Comparing Curriculum Map to Student Achievement	
Purpose	In the previous section, teachers mapped what's taught in their school against what the content and process standards suggest needs to be taught. In this section, participants will compare this standards map to their school data and look for patterns.
Materials Needed	• Copies of disaggregated school achievement data; standardized test data by grade level. • Copies of data recording sheets. • Transparencies of sample data.
Estimated Activity Time	45 minutes

Steps for Facilitation	1. Walking through the data points:
	  a. What kind of info can we derive from the data?
	  b. What does the standard deviation mean?
	  c. Are there any groups that are achieving at lower levels?
	2. Review the data and compare the findings to the curriculum gaps that were discussed in the program mapping section.
	3. Analyze program based on standards and student performance. What is in the standards that we are doing well and/or not doing? What are the strengths and weaknesses of what we are currently doing?
	4. Report by school grade level: What are the strengths and weaknesses of program based on data and standards?

evaluate their curriculum materials objectively. An activity for in-depth curriculum analysis is included in the Resources.

Assessing the Conditions That Support Teacher Collaboration

If teachers are not willing to work together and trust each other, it will be difficult to engage them in the lesson study process. Your own experience as a curriculum leader or principal will help you to know which schools and which teachers might be ready to begin doing lesson study. It may be necessary to try other strategies first, such as forming professional development teams to learn and test a new curriculum. If you facilitate the activities for building understanding of standards, you will probably notice how teachers work together. Assessing the conditions that support teacher collaboration should help you to determine if your school or district can provide the necessary trust, time to meet, facilitative leadership, and strong, agreed-upon content and process goals.

The Voices of Successful Lesson Study Leaders

While preparing this book, we held a number of focus group sessions with educational leaders about how and why they decided to do lesson study, what their experiences had been in doing lesson study, and how it was progressing in their schools and districts. Attending these groups were university professors, preservice teachers, a principal, district curriculum leaders, university and school professional development leaders, and a content specialist involved in lesson study. We analyzed the transcripts of the tapes and looked for emerging themes in relationship to getting started with lesson study. Their voices add substance and subtlety to all the recommendations included in this chapter. They suggest additional essential elements that may be necessary for schools to engage successfully in lesson study.

Passion and Vision

"Passionate" describes the members of our professional development team who make up the New Mexico Learning Collaborative. We are passionate about providing learning opportunities for all students, and in most cases also highly experienced in teaching, professional development, and participation in a number of reform initiatives beginning in the 1970s and 1980s. One recent visitor to a lesson study conference called us the "true believers." Underlying our work is belief in the ability of teachers to teach, design, and assess their classroom activities, as well as a belief that **all children can learn.** In spite of our dissatisfaction with how long it has taken to realize our vision of productive learning communities for teachers and students, we remain full of hope that this will happen. Engaging in lesson study was a significant step in which all children are engaged in productive learning.

It was interesting that in all the focus groups, almost everyone mentioned a book that we had discovered independently during our own periods of dissatisfaction, and that we embraced in various ways: *The Teaching Gap* by James Stigler and James Hiebert (1999). Catherine Lewis (1995) first introduced the idea of lesson study through her book *Educating Hearts and Minds.* However, it was only with *The Teaching Gap* that many of us began to think about lesson study. Perhaps it was the TIMMS study (National Center for Education Statistics, 1999a), showing dramatic differences between Japanese and American students' performance in math and science, that prepared us for a book about a cultural teaching gap that might help explain these differences in achievement. Repeatedly, while we were together in focus groups reflecting on the impact of lesson study, members mentioned reading *The Teaching Gap.*

> I don't think it's coincidental that the teacher group that I brought to that first one [statewide lesson study conference] had read *The Teaching Gap.* If I had said "Do you want to go to a lesson study conference?" and they hadn't read *The Teaching Gap,* I don't think I would have gotten any takers. (Franie Dever, Mathematics Curriculum Leader)

Our individual recollections of when and how we became interested in lesson study all involved some interaction with this book.

> Well, let's see, we've been doing some type of professional development in math for the last six years in this project and four years ago we decided to start thinking about how to do some version of lesson study in the United States because we were pretty dissatisfied with the results of our work . . . And we think we have a philosophy of being collaborative and including whoever we're working with in the process of

designing the professional development . . . And we wanted to move to something that was more about where teachers were at, where they lived, what they did every day. And after reading *The Teaching Gap*, I remember having a conversation with Lisa saying, "Could we do this?" and the first thought was it probably won't work. But we were intrigued by the idea and wanted to figure out a way to think about how it might work in our work, so that was four years [ago] . . . (Wanda Guzman, Mathematics Professional Development Specialist)

I remember it like it was my birthday. In her little sneaky way she had given me this book to read, and I read it. See, she already knew it was going to happen. I said this is amazing and this is what we need to do. And she said yeah I think so too that is why I wanted you to read the book *The Teaching Gap*, and I said we need to do this and she said how can we do it. And we had this conversation; we did say, is this going to work?, probably not. How can we do this, teachers aren't set up to do this here. But we said it doesn't matter, we just got passionate about it. There was something that we just both believed in and our summer institute was coming up and she and I were sort of in charge of planning it and so we said this is what we're going to do. (Lisa Snow, Science/Math Professional Development Specialist)

We could have designed and implemented alternative strategies to empower teachers, such as peer coaching, which is gaining popularity in some school districts, including Boston, Dallas, and Philadelphia (Russo, 2003). In this professional development model, teachers are assigned a "coach" who observes in that teacher's classroom, and together they reflect on the lesson and look at student learning. Other recommended strategies for teacher leaders are included in *Getting Results With Curriculum Mapping* (Jacobs, 2004) as ways for teachers to start understanding and making changes in the curriculum. There have been large efforts to introduce data-based decision making and goal-oriented actions, such as using the Baldridge Model. Yet, all these methods seem to embrace only a part of the problem. Teachers and even instruction are not always the driving forces in these movements; sometimes these efforts don't even touch classrooms or teachers' everyday work. We feel that lesson study provides teachers with more opportunities to gain new knowledge, change attitudes—and more important, to actually change behaviors—through a process of reflection, redesign, and practice. One of our professional development leaders suggested:

> I'm happy with lesson study—it seems like there is so much more to learn and we could get much better at it, and its not a one-size-fits-all, but it's a process that you make work for the population of the teachers of the group that you're working with. I like that; I like the malleability of that.

The lesson study process can be massaged to meet the needs of your teachers in your school district. In fact, the lesson study process, as described in Chapter 4, is grounded in your schoolwide learning goals and the curriculum goals in your district. As we saw in Chapter 1, teachers address these factors and design overarching goals for their students before focusing on their research lesson.

The key for all the participants in this group was the growing understanding that what lesson study must always have is a focus on learning. As you develop a program (times to meet, participants, research lessons developed, measurement of student learning), the professional developer must acknowledge the culture of the schools and work within that culture to make the needed changes that will allow the lesson study process to make a difference in student learning.

Trust

Trust is defined as "confident expectation or hope; honesty, justice" (Thorndike & Barnhart, 1988, p. 1247). Despite the doubts of Wanda Guzman and Lisa Snow, as expressed in their comments above, they succeeded in getting teachers to agree to try lesson study. Both of them believed that the fact that they had been working with these teachers for more than a year was key to getting them to participate in lesson study. There must be trust among the teachers, among the teachers and administrators, and among the professional staff developers, teachers, and administrators. If a university player is involved, it must be as a knowledgeable member or mentor, not only as an "authority" from outside. Lesson study must be based in the school and driven by the teachers.

Teachers need to make the decision to go ahead with lesson study, even when lesson study is introduced by an administrator or curriculum specialist. It is useful to provide teachers with the opportunity to discuss and document how traditional staff development has not translated into improved student learning. Teachers want their students to be successful, as do the administrators. Through discussion and the assessment of teacher readiness, trust can be built, and then the group is much more willing to begin.

Currently, most teachers around the country continue to participate in a more traditional professional development model. If these teachers are going to implement standards-based curricula and foster learning environments where inquiry, communication, and problem solving are key components, then a new, transformative professional development model must be adopted. Such a model involves sweeping changes in deeply held beliefs, knowledge, and habits of practice (Newsome, 2001). Changing teacher beliefs is at the heart of changing the culture of teaching.

One of the participants in this focus group was Susan Brown, also coauthor of this book. She was asked to take over a National Science Foundation (NSF) project from another investigator who had moved away. When Susan, as the new director, and her staff eagerly jumped in with both feet and enthusiastically presented the lesson study concept to the teachers in a summer institute, it fell flat. She later realized that this was the first time she had actually met with the teachers. They had trusted the previous principal investigators (PIs) and may have felt deserted when they went to another university. While Susan presented the research on how something needed to change to help the students, the idea of doing lesson study was not well received. She had not had time to build trust, she hadn't worked closely with the teachers or been in their classrooms, and she hadn't thought about how the teachers might react to change. More than half the teachers did not want change, no matter what the change was to be. They had been comfortable with the previous 2 years and did not want this routine changed.

It is interesting to note that the teachers who were new to the program, having recently moved into the school and joined the team, were the most enthusiastic. The teachers who had received the most attention from the original PIs dug in their heels and put up roadblocks to the new plan. They did not trust the new PIs and definitely would not trust this new method of professional development, no matter what Susan and her staff did. During this year there were a few success stories, but not many. Susan and her staff kept talking with the teachers, building trust. After the first year together, two of the teachers most vehemently opposed to trying lesson study attended a lesson study conference, and they became two of its strongest advocates. The point for the reader is simply that it takes time to develop trust.

Leadership

Another factor in the failure of lesson study to work in a situation that involved new curriculum leadership may have been that the schools and districts, and the administrators with whom the teachers worked, were not ready for change. Lesson study as a district professional development effort will probably not work if the administrators are not on board. As Dennis Sparks writes in an essay (Sparks, 2004):

> The most successful stories related to Lesson Study came from schools where the principal and vice-principals were integral members of the Lesson Study team. By participating, the administration understands the process and the benefits of this process. In one school where there is a strong Lesson Study support by the administration and the teachers, the standardized scores for math jumped from over 70% of the student population being below proficiency to only 23% being below proficiency in mathematics. (p. 106)

Principals across the nation feel that professional development belongs within each school. Who knows best but the administrators and teachers of each individual school how to increase their students' learning? As one principal in our focus group stated:

> The district is right to move resources for professional development to the school. In this way, we can align learning for teachers to the school's goal for student achievement . . . We (teachers and administrators) in the schools want to do a good job, and we want some freedom and to be trusted that we can make good decisions that will increase student achievement.

Principals, with their teachers, can form energetic and powerful teams, leading to changes in student engagement and interactions in classrooms. There are various activities that can be used to introduce teachers to lesson study. One of these is provided in the Resources under Chapter 3.

Conclusion

Chapter 3 provides guidance to potential users of lesson study in terms of whether their school or organization has the capacity to engage in lesson study, or whether they need to take specific steps prior to implementation of such a dramatic and demanding form of professional development. We have provided tools for assessing readiness for change, as well as possible first steps that can be taken to create an environment for lesson study. These include aligning the curriculum, using curriculum mapping, and ensuring that the organization is ready for a new kind of professional development. It is important to remember that lesson study, by itself, cannot change student learning without a schoolwide effort to align teaching, assessment, and the use of quality materials aligned with content standards.

Extended Learning Questions

1. Discuss the different overarching goals that teachers from different schools have developed. What do you think accounts for some of the differences in these goals?

2. Using the MathStar Lesson Planning Template (included in this chapter), begin to fill out the planning portion for your lesson study.

3. If you are doing mathematics lesson study, you might want to follow our example. Pass out and have the participants read the vignettes from *Knowing and Teaching Elementary Mathematics* (Ma, 1999). Note how this teacher reflected on the essential mathematical understandings connected to students learning about multiplying three-digit numbers. Then answer the following questions:
   – What prerequisite understandings must students have?
   – How are the mathematical procedures and concepts related to multiplying three-digit numbers represented in the knowledge packet?
   – How does this knowledge packet influence the planning of the lesson?

Participants should reflect on all these questions and begin designing their own knowledge packets for their own research lesson topics.

4

Connecting Instructional Goals to Lesson Study

Arriving at one goal is the starting point to another.

—John Dewey

Reform must come from within, not from without.

—James Gibbons

Our state holds an annual lesson study conference in conjunction with our annual mathematics and science conference. In addition to providing opportunities for teams to present and share their lessons and findings, the purpose of the annual state conference is also to learn new skills needed to participate in lesson study. During the most recent conference, we decided to focus on two components of the lesson study process that we found to be weak areas for many teams. The first focal point, which we discuss in this chapter, involves developing and integrating the overarching goal, connecting it to your school's instructional goals, and then connecting the research lesson to a larger unit goal. The second focal point—anticipating student thinking as part of designing the research lesson—is discussed in Chapter 5.

We have seen the difference that including the overarching goal makes in connecting classroom lesson study to the overall instructional goals and mission of the school. Particularly for schools that are designated in need of improvement because of the No Child Left Behind (NCLB) legislation, it is essential that all educational change efforts be tied directly to the instructional goals of the school, which should be based on students' learning needs.

This chapter is about goals: the overarching goal that teachers and administrators have for their students as people; the content area goal, in which teachers think about what it means to do math or science or another content area; and the unit goal, namely what you want students to learn and understand. All these goals relate to each other and to your plan for the research lesson.

As we conducted focus groups and interviews with the major lesson study players in New Mexico, Arizona, and Texas, one of the interesting behaviors we observed was the tendency of lesson study leaders and teams to move back and forth between discussions of the curriculum, the need for improving student achievement and performance, and the need to help teachers improve their practice. Goal setting is the critical component of lesson study that ties all these efforts together. As you start on your own lesson study journey, it is important to take the time to answer the first critical question: What kind of people do you want your students to be when they leave your school?

Developing the Overarching Goal

Over the years we have designed some strategies that can help teams to develop their overarching goal for lesson study. The exercise included in Table 4.A asks teachers to begin designing their overarching goal by thinking about what the ideal students might look like, what characteristics students might have now in relationship to the ideal, and how you might close the gap between desired characteristics and reality.

It is important to provide time for teachers to do the following exercise individually. First, before building a community it is necessary to develop consensus in relationship to the overarching goal. Providing time for individual teachers to share their ideas during workshops allows participants to bring their own meaning and experience to the task and increases the meaningfulness of the professional development experience.

Table 4.A   Teacher Collaborative Study Groups

Exercise I: Developing Overarching Goals	
Purpose	The purpose of this activity is to provide you, as a teacher, an opportunity to think about the students you serve and what you would like them to be as people in the future.
Your ideals	What qualities would you like your students to have 5 years from now?
The Actual	List the qualities they have now in relationship to the ideals.
The Gap	Compare the ideal and the actual. Determine for yourself which gaps you would most likely want to work on closing. State positively the ideal student qualities you would like to work on.

After teachers have had the opportunity to work individually, provide time for teacher teams to share and facilitate brainstorming the goals of each school group. This usually involves writing everyone's ideas from a specific school or project on a board or large paper, and then working to combine some of the student characteristics into a single goal statement. Keep asking the group members for their agreement on how they want to express their most important ideas. Be sure to get agreement on language before moving on.

Sample Goals From Other Lesson Study Groups

Here are some goals that different lesson study groups have chosen:

- Students will become confident in their ability to learn.
- Students will become independent thinkers and be able to work together to facilitate creative solutions to problems.
- Students will become confident in applying math to other areas of the curriculum.
- Students will become confident in their ability to use and integrate technology into their student work.
- Students will be risk takers and think outside the box in all areas of the curriculum.

- Students will be critical thinkers; they will be able to analyze data and draw conclusions.
- Students will work together, share ideas, respect one another, and use these skills to solve problems.

Schools throughout the country are working to set their own specific goals in relation to their education plans for student success. Both professional development and instructional goals in a school should relate to these required whole-school goals. In our state we have what is called the EPSS (Educational Plan for Student Success). We have found that this is the easiest way to connect the whole-school mission to small teacher teams for lesson study.

For example, in Las Cruces, the mission of the entire school district is:

> The Las Cruces Public Schools community is committed to an environment which the district's children will have an education resulting in greater student performance, academic achievement, and higher self-esteem and respect for themselves and others.

The mission statement for Lynn Middle School is:

> The mission of Lynn Middle School is to create a safe and positive learning environment for all students. All students will be challenged with a strong academic program in all content areas, with an emphasis in reading comprehension skills. Students will learn to appreciate and celebrate diversity while maintaining a strong sense of self-worth and responsibility. We will actively seek the vital collaboration and support of parent and community partnership to accomplish this mission.

A study by Mike Schmoker (1999) establishes the importance of setting district and whole-school goals. "Goals themselves lead not only to success but also to the effectiveness and cohesion of a team" (p. 24). In the Las Cruces district, each school expands the mission statement to cite specific goals that the school will achieve for the new school year. For example, three of the specific goals for Lynn from last year included:

1. To increase the math achievement of Lynn students to exceed state standards.

2. To increase the science achievement of Lynn students to exceed state standards.

3. To maintain/increase the student attendance rate to meet or exceed the exemplary state standards.

The objective for the research lesson established by the staff team of Lynn Middle School states:

The goal of this lesson is to build confidence and expertise in the students to use the Excel program, and the use of problem solving as they work within a group.

This lesson fits within the district's mission, the school's mission, and the specific goals set by the teachers of Lynn Middle School. Through their work in groups, the students gain confidence and respect for one another while building knowledge in collecting data, designing graphs to illustrate this data, and then interpreting the data. All this work is ultimately increasing math and science achievement, while the use of the software and graphing techniques can be applied to other curricular areas.

Developing Content Area Goals

Lesson study provides an opportunity for teachers to think about what it means to learn an academic content area. Every content area has key components involving process and content that constitute the nature of disciplinary learning. While there are whole manuals related to the standards and core ideas of each academic discipline, a useful exercise is to consider what is at the core of the discipline. The following are some core ideas that have been offered in different workshops about the structure and process of a discipline. You might want to divide teachers by their disciplinary areas and ask them what they think are the key characteristics of the subject they teach. Here are some sample descriptions of different disciplines:

- Literacy involves the skillful interaction of reading, writing, and speaking, as students attempt to make meaning of text.
- Social studies requires understanding relationships between citizens and their political, economic, and geographic environments, as well as relationships between different countries and the world.
- Science is grounded in the process of inquiry and a growing understanding of the physical world.
- Mathematics is a way to describe relationships between numbers of things.

The Content Standards

In addition to reflecting on their own experiences of teaching an academic discipline, teachers can use the standards developed by national professional organizations to understand the core ideas of a content area, as well as the process skills that help students deepen their knowledge in that discipline.

However, we suggest caution when working with standards. We've seen too many situations in which teachers are required to copy and paste district or state standards into their lessons, sometimes simply recording the numbers of the standards, without considering the essential ideas that students need to understand to master the subject. We usually introduce standards by asking teachers to define for themselves what are the "big ideas" in the standards, the ideas that students need to understand in a discipline in order to know that discipline. This might be coached in any of the following ways:

- Imagine that, during the summer, you happen to run into two of your students from your science (or other subject) class at the mall. If you asked them what they remembered from your class, what would you want them to say? What one or two critical ideas would you expect them to remember and be able to share with you?
- Suppose your eighth-grade math class was the last math class that a student would ever take. What key ideas about mathematics would you want students to take with them into adult life?

Elliot Eisner (1994) suggests that education is what you know after you have left school. It is not simply the memorization of facts that may be easily forgotten, but a deeper understanding, or a way to think about ideas that lasts beyond the final exam. Ideas like the following might be topics for conversations among groups of teachers: *What does it mean to be educated in your field? What do you want students to know and be able to do by studying a discipline? What do you want students to understand deeply enough that they take that understanding with them to the next grade and into their lives?*

In our experience, it is important that teachers be introduced to standards in terms of the big ideas they represent and not be encouraged to participate in the rote copying of standard numbers into their lesson plans. Comparing standards that students should know and be able to demonstrate with actual test performance in relation to these standards is another way to begin to define what learning gaps you might want to address in your research lesson. For your second-level goal, it is significant to answer the question of what it means for your students to be mathematicians or readers or writers or scientists. How students learn to deeply understand the main concepts in a discipline is often related to how these ideas are taught. Most teachers are familiar with Bloom's taxonomy and how to ask questions that lead to higher-level thinking. You might want to create a chart such as the following to help teachers think about how they teach standards.

In order to provide scaffolding for goal development in lesson study, we have created a template for developing a research lesson. In this chapter we introduce you to the first part of this template, which involves planning the goals within which your research lesson will be developed. The four levels of goals can also be seen in terms of circles around the core activity of conducting the research lesson. In Chapter 5, we discuss the rest of the research lesson process.

The unit goal should connect your ultimate research lesson to the larger goals, including your goal for content learning and the overarching goal within which you are planning your research lesson. Research lessons are not very useful if they are isolated learning activities and not connected to the curriculum you are providing to students. A research lesson is a window into an area of learning, and we have found that it needs to be related to the larger unit goal. As part of this process, we teach teachers a simplified version of the backwards design process developed by the authors of *Understanding by Design* (Wiggins & McTighe, 1998).

There are two reasons to do this. First, focusing on lessons as part of helping students to gain an understanding of something larger and core to the school curriculum helps teachers break away from traditional lesson planning. Traditional lesson planning has often been seen as just listing a series of activities that students will do. Time spent on what you want students to understand and how you will assess this understanding is time well spent.

Second, grounding lesson study in the larger context of curriculum goals keeps teachers from wanting to do a "cute" lesson that is really unrelated to the school's larger learning needs and overarching goals. In an era when teachers simply have too much to do, energy must be focused on the most important things that the students in your school need to learn.

We use two resources in working with lesson study teams on unit design. The first book is Wiggins and McTighe's (1998) *Understanding by Design*. In addition, these authors have available accompanying workbooks and Web-based materials. The second resource we use for backwards design is the Teaching for Understanding Project at

(Text continues on page 74)

Seventh-Grade Mathematics Standards

Strand 1: NUMBER AND OPERATIONS
Standard: Students will understand numerical concepts and mathematical operations.

Mathematics Benchmarks and Performance Standards	Expectations for Students in Mathematics				
	Mathematics Skills		Problem Solving		
	Recall Information	Apply Procedural Knowledge	Communicate & Represent Understanding	Analyze, Reason, & Prove	Make Connections & Evaluate
5–8 Benchmark 1: Understand numbers, ways of representing numbers, relationships among numbers, and number systems.	*Time Spent in Each Performance Standard* *Indicate N (never), S (sometimes), or U (usually) for each expectation*				
Performance Standards					
1. Determine the absolute value of rational numbers.					
2. Illustrate the relationships among natural (i.e., counting) numbers, whole numbers, integers, and rational and irrational numbers.					

Strand 1: NUMBER AND OPERATIONS

Standard: Students will understand numerical concepts and mathematical operations.

Mathematics Benchmarks and Performance Standards	Expectations for Students in Mathematics				
	Mathematics Skills		Problem Solving		
	Recall Information	Apply Procedural Knowledge	Communicate & Represent Understanding	Analyze, Reason, & Prove	Make Connections & Evaluate
5–8 Benchmark 2: Understands the meaning of operations and how they relate to one another.	*Time Spent in Each Performance Standard* *Indicate* **N** *(never),* **S** *(sometimes), or* **U** *(usually) for each expectation*				
3. Use properties of the real number system to explain reasoning and to formulate and solve real-world problems.					
4. Read, write, and compare rational numbers in scientific notation (e.g., positive and negative powers of 10) with approximate numbers using scientific notation.					
Simplify numerical expressions using order of operations.					

(Continued)

Strand 1: NUMBER AND OPERATIONS

Standard: Students will understand numerical concepts and mathematical operations.

Mathematics Benchmarks and Performance Standards	Expectations for Students in Mathematics				
	Mathematics Skills		**Problem Solving**		
	Recall Information	Apply Procedural Knowledge	Communicate & Represent Understanding	Analyze, Reason, & Prove	Make Connections & Evaluate
Performance Standards					
1. Add, subtract, multiply, and divide rational numbers (e.g., integers, fractions, terminating decimals) and take positive rational numbers to whole-number powers.					
2. Convert terminating decimals into reduced fractions.					
3. Calculate given percentages of quantities and use them to solve problems (e.g., discounts of sales, interest earned, tips, markups, commission, profit, and simple interest).					
4. Add and subtract fractions with unlike denominators.					
5. Multiply, divide, and simplify rational numbers by using exponent rules.					

Strand 1: NUMBER AND OPERATIONS

Standard: Students will understand numerical concepts and mathematical operations.

Mathematics Benchmarks and Performance Standards	Expectations for Students in Mathematics				
	Mathematics Skills		Problem Solving		
	Recall Information	Apply Procedural Knowledge	Communicate & Represent Understanding	Analyze, Reason, & Prove	Make Connections & Evaluate
5–8 Benchmark 3: Compute fluently and make reasonable estimates.	*Time Spent in Each Performance Standard* — *Indicate* **N** *(never),* **S** *(sometimes), or* **U** *(usually) for each expectation*				
6. Understand the meaning of the absolute value of a number: a. Interpret the absolute value as the distance of the number from zero on a number line. b. Determine the absolute values of real numbers.					
7. Find square roots of perfect whole–number squares.					
8. Simplify and evaluate positive rational numbers raised to positive whole-number powers.					
9. Solve addition, subtraction, multiplication, and division problems that use positive and negative integers and combinations of these operations.					

(Continued)

Strand 1: NUMBER AND OPERATIONS

Standard: Students will understand numerical concepts and mathematical operations.

Mathematics Benchmarks and Performance Standards	Expectations for Students in Mathematics				
	Mathematics Skills		Problem Solving		
	Recall Information	Apply Procedural Knowledge	Communicate & Represent Understanding	Analyze, Reason, & Prove	Make Connections & Evaluate
Performance Standards					
1. Use estimation to check reasonableness of results, and use this information to make predictions in situations involving rational numbers, pi, and simple algebraic equations.					
2. Convert fractions to decimals and percents and use these representations in estimations, computations, and applications.					
3. Read, write, and compare rational numbers in scientific notation (e.g., positive and negative powers of 10) with approximate numbers using scientific notation.					
4. Calculate the percentage of increases and decreases of a quantity.					
5. Add and subtract fractions with unlike denominators.					
6. Use the inverse relationship between raising to a power and extracting the root of a perfect square integer.					

Research Lesson Template

Grade Level: **Date:**

Instructor: **# of Students:**

Class Time: **Class Type (check one):**

Location: ☐ Regular ☐ SPED ☐ Bilingual/ESL ☐ Other

Comments: *Describe social and cultural context of school.*

I. Goals:

  A. Overarching Goal: (*What kinds of people do you want your students to be?*)

  B. Content Goal: (*What kinds of mathematicians do you want your students to be?*)

  C. Unit Goals: (*What are your math goals for your students as a result of doing this unit?*)

Overarching Lesson Study Goal

Content Goal

Unit Goal

Research Lesson Goal

II. Description of Unit:
  (One or two sentences)

  A. How does this lesson fit into the unit?

  B. Previously learned concepts: (*What concepts are needed to do this lesson?*)

  C. Concepts to be learned in this lesson:

Harvard (see http://www.pz.harvard.edu/Research/TfU.htm). There are excellent activities available online that include supplementary resource materials for backwards planning. Like spending time on overarching goals, the time spent in helping teachers rethink content in terms of student understanding is well worth the effort. The lesson needs to flow from these larger contexts. Take the time to fully develop and complete the lesson planning circle.

Knowledge Packets

At this point, you want to provide resources for conceptualizing core ideas in the content area in which your teachers plan to conduct their lesson study. Graphical organizers can be helpful and can either be provided or teachers can generate their own pictures of knowledge to be learned using software such as Inspiration (www.inspiration.com) or simply felt-tip pens and large sheets of paper. One example of knowledge organization we borrowed for mathematics lesson study came from the work of Liping Ma (1999), who suggested the term *knowledge packet* for planning for teaching a key concept. She suggests that teachers might want to create a knowledge packet related to the different kinds of knowledge that lead to a core under-standing, such as what it means to multiply. In her book she presents a picture of the key concept to be taught and the relationship of this content to prerequisite knowledge and skills, including related content. Regardless of the content area, using some kind of graphical organizer is helpful in defining the unit and eventually the lesson within that unit, which will be central to the research lesson.

The Unit Planning Process

We utilized a very simplified unit planning design in our workshops. The following plan provides a scenario for a two-day workshop. The workshop can be broken up into shorter sessions over a longer period of time, based on what kind of professional development time is available in a school or district. A complete guide to the unit planning workshop is included in the Resources.

Why Spend So Much Time on Planning?

You may be wondering why we are spending so much time on goals and unit planning. We believe that it is only by changing the culture of teaching in a movement lead by teachers—a lesson study movement—that we can provide increased opportunities for learning for all students. Multiple reform efforts have often been unsuccessful in decreasing the achievement gap between our high-achieving and low-achieving students. Our experience in conducting professional development for many years, as well as our success with lesson study, has convinced us that we should not continue to do more of the same. Instead, we must help teachers develop a deep understanding of what it means to facilitate student learning. Teaching by delivering information has been the dominant mode of instruction in the United States. This method has not worked to help numerous students, especially non-mainstream students, to increase their learning or achievement in schools. In fact, the latest National Assessment of Educational Progress (2004) data indicate that the gap between mainstream students and economically poor and culturally diverse students is growing. Professional development modeled on telling teachers what to do is no more successful than teachers telling their students what to do.

The current culture of teaching is deeply rooted in providing students with activities and answers. When videotaping teachers in their first cycle or two of lesson study, we observed—and more important, the teachers observed—how much they want to give students all the answers. But giving students all the answers, especially for students who lack their own learning skills, will not solve the achievement problem in the United States. For some reason, teachers are uncomfortable with asking students to find the answers on their own. Perhaps one of the roots of the problem is that teachers have been asked to develop lesson plans that are descriptions of learning activities the teacher will provide and direct. What we are suggesting in this chapter is that teachers need to think differently about teaching before they can facilitate learning for all students.

The unit planning process is one tool that helps teachers to think differently about teaching. We are suggesting that teachers first decide what it is they want the students to understand, then how to assess that understanding, and finally how to design learning activities that will facilitate understanding. The need is to shift their focus from what they will teach or tell to what will help the students to understand and learn. In every lesson study experience that we have monitored, teachers usually have several breakthrough experiences. Primarily, they realize how anxious they are to tell students the answers. In our early work with teachers and lesson study, we simply suggested that teachers take the students' question and turn it into a question for the students. This turned out to be a good way for teachers to ask their students to put more energy into the learning process. Teachers learned to ask students to explain the problem to them, to tell them what they had tried, to ask them what they know so far, and so on.

The second breakthrough we observed is that at some point in the process teachers have an "aha!" moment related to teaching and learning. They suddenly realize that more learning happens when the students are given more responsibility for the learning. Some teachers recognize this as how they have not used the resources in their own classrooms, namely the students themselves. One teacher commented that she suddenly realized that she had 25 other teachers in her classroom. For all these reasons, it is vital that you spend additional time on the unit planning process.

Assessment of Student Understanding

This workshop on assessment is a combination of having teachers think about assessment and what they know about it, while also observing a variety of open-ended assessment problems in their content areas. We might begin such a workshop by having teachers take a blank piece of paper and draw the word "assessment" in a circle in the center of the paper. We then provide teachers with time to add words and ideas related to what they currently know about assessment. At the end of the day or after several short sessions, teachers can be given back the same paper, and in a different color ink, add what they now know about assessment. This is an excellent assessment tool for the presenters as well, since they now know something about what the teachers have learned.

Part I—Working With Balanced Assessment Items

Part I of this workshop involves presenting teachers with a variety of different open-ended assessments such as those often offered in new kinds of standardized testing, based on measuring students' deep understanding of a problem. The following is an example of assessment items from testing companies:

Several notions of assessment are developed with the group. This section of the workshop begins by having everyone solve an assessment involving probability, doing the task themselves, talking about how they would assess the task, and then looking at and evaluating sample student work. A discussion of types and purposes of assessment should follow this. Small groups will have time to begin working on a simple student assessment for the final week of teaching.

Pet Food

> **This problem gives you the chance to:**
> *Apply numbers and simple fractions
> in a real context*

Ricardo has one cat called Mew-Mew and two dogs called Sparky and Buster. The chart below shows how much dry food each animal eats in a day.

Mew-Mew	¼ pound of dry cat food
Sparky	¾ pound of dry dog food
Buster	¾ pound of dry dog food

Should Ricardo buy these bags of food for his pets?

Which kind of food will get used up first?

Show or describe how you figured out which kind of food will be used up first.

_____

_____

_____

_____

_____

Part II—Developing Assessment for Lesson Study

While teachers have some ideas about what students do not understand, they do not always have a deep understanding of exactly what a student can and cannot do in relationship to understanding a concept. Before teachers begin to develop a research lesson, it is often helpful for them to assess their own students in an area that they are considering for planning a research lesson. Here is one example from our work with high school math teachers. Many of the high school teachers felt their students were still having trouble with the computation of fractions. We suggested that the teachers design an assessment that determines just where that understanding breaks down.

Pet Food Rubric		
The core elements of performance required by this task are: • *Apply numbers and simple fractions in a real context.* Based on this, credit for specific aspects of performance should be assigned as follows:	**Points**	**Section Points**
Calculates or explains that the cat food will last for 40 days *Partial credit:* Score as one point trying to find how many ¼s there are in 10, but not carrying it through to the correct answer.	2 (1)	2
Calculates or explains that the dog food will last for Between 33 and 34 days *Partial credit:* • Score as one point showing that each day 1½ pounds are used. • Score as one point the attempt to find how many 1½s there are in 50.	3 (1) (1)	3
If there is no summary statement, or an incorrect conclusion, subtract one point from total score. *(Minimum score for question is 0.)*	0	0
Total Points		5

In other words, do the students really understand what a fraction is? In the sample assessment, students were asked to draw and color in fractions. We were all very surprised when several students demonstrated in their assessment that they had forgotten the notion that fractions involve dividing things into equal parts.

Table 4.B provides a quick overview of the four levels of goals.

The Research Lesson Goal

The last goal we want to discuss is the specific goal that teachers develop in relation to the research lesson. This goal is often based on a question about what students will be learning during the research lesson. The best way to facilitate the research lesson goal is to make sure that teachers have an understanding of what is a good research question.

Table 4.B   A Quick Overview of the Four Levels of Goals

Level One	*Overarching goals* **are long-term goals for student development.** *What kinds of people do you want your students to be?*
Level Two	*Subject-matter goals* **relate to the discipline(s) you teach.** *(For example. what qualities do mathematics learners need to have?)*
Level Three	*Unit goals* **relate to the main content and process standards for which you have found learning.** *At the end of this unit, your students should gain understanding and appreciation of what essential content and processes?*
Level Four	*Lesson goals* **relate to a critical lesson within the unit that you are focusing on.** *What lesson(s) can we plan, facilitate, and study that can be used during the unit to really help students gain essential understandings? What instructional strategies will assist students in gaining this understanding?*

When we first introduced lesson study to teachers in our math project 4 years ago, we decided to ground lesson study in teacher action research. Both authors participated in action research as early as 1980 (Wiburg & Fernandez, 1993) and recognize that lesson study fits very well into a long-standing American tradition of teacher research and reflection on practice. Teacher research has been a powerful force in improving instruction in several schools and districts. One of the best resources for teacher action research and specifically teacher *collaborative* action research is the work of Richard Sagor (1992). His easy-to-understand book on how to do teacher action research is available from the Association for Supervision and Curriculum Development (www.ascd.org). Recently, Sagor (2004) published a new book on how to connect action research with school reform. This book extends one of the themes of this chapter—the importance of connecting teacher study with the larger learning needs of students in a school.

When teachers first hear the word *research*, they often feel intimidated and imagine research projects they were once asked to do in college graduate programs involving extensive statistics and difficult reading. It is important for teachers to come to see themselves as the researchers they really are when they design and deliver lessons in their classrooms. Experienced teachers have a deep and intuitive understanding of what students know and need, and they must be supported in expressing and appreciating this understanding. It is important to the discussion of research to ask teachers what they are curious about in terms of student learning. This might involve asking them to think of concepts that students have trouble understanding and then asking them to suggest alternative reasons for why students might not understand, then following up by proposing what they might try to do to find out what kind of teaching approach might help the students understand better.

Action Research and the Professional Development Plan

Recently, we were invited into a district to assist the administrators and teachers in meeting the professional development plans that are currently required in many states. The superintendent for instruction was familiar with our action research from previous professional development efforts, and decided that action research was the perfect answer to how teachers can meet the state requirements for a professional development plan. The state and district plan required teachers to do some type of professional development that would directly affect student instructional needs. The district helped facilitate thinking about instruction in core areas by asking all schools to address only two major goals in all professional development and instructional reform. Improving literacy and enhancing mathematical learning formed the core educational plan for student success goals. Accordingly, all teachers had to include in their action research plan some activity related to numbers, reading, writing, listening, and speaking. Given this, the teachers met in subject area groups and worked for an afternoon to develop their research question and what they would do to answer their question. We told them that they could ask and answer only one question in relationship to one instructional area. They needed to specify the content standard they were addressing, the research question they would ask, and how they would gather data to answer the question.

Several schools that already had well-developed teams created plans quickly. (See Chapters 2 and 5 for more information on building professional communities.) For example, one middle school science department group met with their cross-disciplinary team (math, English, social studies) and decided they wanted to address their students' lack of comprehension in reading. They determined that they would attempt to increase the use of science vocabulary among all their students in all core subject areas. They agreed to pretest their students on science vocabulary words by asking students to draw a picture and write a sentence about a vocabulary word. They would all use the same vocabulary words in all their classes for 3 weeks, introducing 10 new words each week. After a month or so, they would post-test the students to see if their collaborative instructional plan was increasing students' comprehension of science vocabulary.

This is just one example of the innovative ideas that teachers come up with in researching and their students' learning. In a recent focus group, a lesson study facilitator for a large urban district discussed how some of her school groups were having trouble with lesson study and the research lesson. She remarked as follows:

> . . . I'm trying to figure out how some schools are maintaining. Of those five I think there are four who said that they are doing it. Some already did do it. One school. with very little support, has just embraced this, and I'm not . . . I mean they have an instructional coach who is organizing them, but in terms of coming together, meetings that my intuition tells me fuel these kinds of projects that social learning theory, sense of community, having to present all of that. Without that, I was expecting even more attrition. But there are at least five sites that are continuing on, but it's not the same people. You know I'm wondering about that, you know, who gets hooked? And I think that in the culture of the school it can drift from sets to sets and stay alive, but I'm not sure. I know that leadership is needed somewhere.

Conclusion

Setting goals makes a difference! Lipsey and Wilson (1993) examined 204 different studies and found that, when teachers set academic goals, the achievement scores in classes in which clear learning goals were established were 0.55 standard deviation higher than the achievement scores for classes in which clear learning goals were not established. Through the lesson study process, the teachers use goals already established by the district and the individual school to guide their lessons and establish academic goals for the overarching unit, the specific subject matter, the unit, and the specific lessons. Goals facilitate the actual lesson development and, in turn, become a catalyst for increasing the academic achievement of the students within those classrooms.

Extended Learning Questions

1. Discuss the different overarching goals that teachers from different schools have developed. What do you think accounts for some of the differences in these goals?

2. Using the MathStar Lesson Planning Template (included in this chapter) begin to fill out the planning portion for your lesson study.

3. If you are doing mathematics lesson study, you might want to follow our example. Have the participants read the vignettes from *Knowing and Teaching Elementary Mathematics* (Ma, 1999). Note how this teacher reflected on the essential mathematical understandings connected to students learning about multiplying three-digit numbers. Then answer the following questions:
   - What prerequisite understandings must students have?
   - How are the mathematical procedures and concepts related to multiplying three-digit numbers represented in the knowledge packet?
   - How does this knowledge packet influence the planning of the lesson?

   Participants should reflect on all these questions and begin designing their own knowledge packet for their own research lesson topic.

5

Designing the Research Lesson

Learning is the discovery that something is possible.

—Fritz Perls

Chapters 1 through 4 have provided a rich context for the development of the research lesson. The research lesson itself, which some groups also call the *study lesson* (Fernandez, 2003), is the window into the larger lesson study process. Through this window, teacher groups will share how they are working together to improve learning for students in their classrooms.

Developing the research lesson comes only after teachers, often with the help of their instructional coaches, have developed the overarching goal for their students, their goal for student learning in the targeted content area, and their goal for the unit from which the research lesson is drawn. The content of the research lesson might have been chosen to address what students are having trouble learning, as determined by analysis of student test results, as well as teacher observation and discussion. Such a research lesson might look specifically at the many misperceptions students have about a concept, such as fractions, and be designed to investigate a new way of teaching fractions so that students might have less trouble learning them. The research lesson might also be chosen to address one of the behaviors related to the overarching school goal. For example, if the overarching goal suggests that students work together to solve problems, but group learning continues to present problems in the classroom, the teachers might design a lesson that provides new processes for students to use for group problem solving work.

Teachers will work collaboratively to design the research lesson. This may take some time. Teachers discuss and decide what they want the students to learn from the lesson; what they want to learn from the lesson; and how this lesson demonstrates the important ideas and standards that are the goal of the unit from which the lesson is given. They also examine carefully how this lesson meets the larger overarching goal developed for the school.

Before Planning the Research Lesson

Before the teachers begin to design a research lesson, it is important for teachers to understand the complexity of planning and facilitating lessons that truly focus on student thinking and problem solving (Delisle, 1997). Modern Japanese lesson study, like its evolving practice in the United States, is grounded in inquiry learning and the creation of opportunities for students to engage in problem solving and discussion. Teachers must be familiar with an inquiry, constructivist approach to learning (Marlowe & Page, 1998). In order to design a lesson so that students have opportunities to construct meaning, teachers must be familiar with and comfortable with problem-centered learning. A short review or even a longer session of working with problem-centered learning design is an excellent idea. In other words, in problem-centered, or constructivist, learning, students explore and then learn a concept as a result of the teachers designing a lesson that helps the students to construct meaning. Wenglinsky (2004) compared the effectiveness on student achievement of teaching mathematics for meaning with that of teaching mathematics as the memorization of basic skills, as measured in The National Assessment of Educational Progress (NAEP). The overall results of his study suggest that instruction that emphasizes reasoning skills, critical thinking, and meaning promotes student achievement. While it would be wonderful if knowledge could simply be transferred from the teacher to the student, learning does not always happen this way, especially if we want students to retain and be able to apply what they learn. For students to gain the kind of deep understanding that allows them to build conceptual frameworks in content areas, they must have the opportunity to connect prior knowledge with new understandings through a well-designed, problem-centered learning environment. It is important for the teacher to provide a learning environment that encourages students to make meaning and gain true understanding (Branson, Brown, & Cocking 1999; Gollub, Bertenthal, Labov, & Curtis, 2002).

Designing Problem-Centered Learning

Norton and Wiburg (1998/2002) introduced the notion of a problem-centered curriculum in their book *Teaching With Technology.* They believe that the power of computers to help students learn is tapped only when the computer becomes a support for a constructivist-based model of learning. The problem-centered model for learning is summarized in this chapter, because lesson study works best when it is grounded in a learning-as-inquiry approach. This is equally true in Japanese lesson study, which is also based on creating opportunities for inquiry. The problem-centered model suggests three steps for designing learning opportunities for students.

The first step is to introduce and then help students to further define the problem. This often involves developing questions that are essential to answer as part of solving the problem. In lesson study terminology, this is part of the *launch.* The second stage is to help students build a knowledge base related to the problem through the exploration of and sharing of print and electronic resources, simulations, presentations, and discussions. During this period of *exploration and sharing,* it is necessary for the teacher to act as a facilitator and provide the students with the additional time, resources, and necessary scaffolding to answer the essential questions posed by the initial problem. Finally, as part of *closure,* the teacher needs to help the students to evaluate and possibly modify their alternative solutions to problems and to reflect on and evaluate their own learning until the teacher is sure that the students truly understand the concepts.

In order to illustrate how problem-centered learning might look, we'll share one example from a book by Butler-Pascoe and Wiburg (2003) on using problem-centered instruction to teach science to English Language Learners.

Susan Brown's Middle School Science Classroom: A Classroom Vignette

Sierra Middle School is located in a low- to middle-income city near the border between New Mexico, Texas, and Mexico. The school district in which it is located is about 60 percent Hispanic, and for around 40 percent of the district's students English is not their home language. Sierra is located in an especially poor area of the border city but has been successful over the last 5 years in turning what had once been a gang and problem school into an institution that exemplifies the best of middle school teaching. All the teachers work in teams, and the school day has been restructured so that the teacher teams can meet for planning each day. The curriculum emphasizes thematic teaching and close coordination between each student's regular and resource teachers and parents, with a focus on meeting each student's individual needs.

Susan Brown has taught school for more than 17 years and was one of the middle school science teachers at Sierra who welcomed English Language Learners into her classroom. She has a well-developed instructional approach to teaching science that is successful even with the students from her middle school's Newcomer Center for monolingual Spanish speakers. She uses a project-based approach to science teaching and insists that all students engage in inquiry as they learn science.

Early in the fall, when students first enter her room, they notice a sign that indicates that they are entering the Sierra Sands Scientific Company. Below the sign is an employee manual for each student that states:

> We are proud to welcome you as a new employee to our company. The Sierra Sands Scientific Company is committed to excellence in science education. As a new employee you must complete each of the center activities to ensure that you are familiar with all the scientific equipment we sell to the schools. Again, welcome! We are so excited to have you as a member of our team! (Susan Brown, student manual, Sierra Middle School, 1999)

Susan has carefully constructed centers in which the students will become familiar with the pieces of equipment used in science, including tools for experimentation, computer software, and calculators. In this first project-based activity she asks students to work in pairs and provides enough centers that there is always one available for a pair to work in. She also pulls half the class at a time into an orientation and discussion group with her during each period. She knows that for many students, especially her monolingual Spanish speakers from nearby Mexico, a special orientation to the way in which she teaches science is necessary. In fact, as an experienced teacher, she follows the principle that one should never assume that students know something.

Recently Susan shared with us how a group of Newcomer students entered her room last fall, wide-eyed and afraid to touch things, and yet how quickly these same students became excited and motivated learners once they had experienced success at a center or two. She also talked about how her students from Mexico were often better at estimating than her regular students and definitely better at using metric measures, which are standard in their country.

There are 16 different centers in this introductory science session in Susan's classroom. Some involve simple tasks that teach basic science experiment tools. Students are asked to measure colored water in a beaker; to look at slides under a microscope and a magnifying lens and sketch what they see; to filter tea leaves from a cup of tea and to weigh them; to measure the temperatures of different colored boxes; and to simply measure and weigh objects using the metric system. They are also invited to do a variety of different simple experiments, such as float a boat, discover mystery powders, or investigate the properties of mystery liquids using Petri dishes and test tubes. Some of the centers include using computers for graphing and accessing resources on the Web and using calculators for computation and graphing. Many of the key scientific words and procedures are provided in Spanish in this classroom, but, more important, the manual contains multiple pictures and diagrams that help all students be successful in the centers.

Susan tells the story of one Spanish-speaking student from Mexico who figured out a better way to measure the room than using a meter stick along the sides. She had figured out that because the room had tiles on the floor, all you had to do was measure one tile and then multiply this measurement by the number of tiles along the wall. The student was using body language and kept saying "Uno, dos, tres," while pointing at the tiles. Finally the students in the room got it! It was an incredible learning moment as other groups measuring the room quickly adopted the girl's suggestion.

Professional Development Activity: Practice With Problem-Based Planning

1. Pick a concept of process standard from the standards you are required to teach. Then design a problem-centered approach to teaching one of these standards.

2. Discuss some of the complexities of providing a problem-centered curriculum, especially when working with diverse students who may have different levels of language and ability.

A complete problem-centered science unit on digestion is included in the Resources For Chapter 5. This might be useful in helping teachers to design an inquiry learning environment.

Tools for Designing the Research Problem

It is during the planning of the research lesson that we have found the tools and templates developed to support lesson study so valuable. In Chapter 3, the need for teachers to understand and engage in unit planning prior to the development of the research lesson is emphasized. In this chapter we have explicitly introduced the notion of problem-centered or problem-based learning as a key construct underlying both Japanese and American research lessons. The template we have developed to help teacher teams design the research lesson has two parts. The first part provides the context for the lesson and includes the four levels of goals involved, the unit plan, and the specific standards and concepts that are addressed in the unit. Finally it introduces the research lesson as a window into the unit and the lesson study process. This concept was discussed in Chapter 3, where we introduced the planning component for the research lesson.

In order to help the reader understand how this first part might look, we've included two examples of filled-out Part I forms from actual lesson studies done during our MathStar project. Figure 1 is a research lesson on understanding the meaning of variables in algebra through the use of concrete examples. Figure 2 describes a lesson study on learning large numbers, which involves students in organizing the sizes of planets. The lesson was done at the fifth- and sixth-grade levels in a small rural school district in which cows outnumber people!

Previewing the Design of the Research Lesson

It is now time for the lesson study group to develop the research lesson. In our years of doing lesson study the template provided (see Table 5.A on page 92) has been changed and changed and changed yet again, as it has been used and tested by many groups of teachers.

Figure 1

Research Lesson on Understanding Variables—Part I

Grade Level: 8

Instructor: Jessica Gordon

Class Time: 10:10–11:50

Location:
Harrison Middle School
3912 Isleta Blvd.
Albuquerque, NM 87105
Room E-2

Date: 4/15/03

# of Students: 24

Class Type (check one):

☐ Regular   ☐ SPED   ☐ Bilingual/ESL   ☐ Other

Comments: *(Describe social cultural context of school)*
Harrison's student population is 85 percent Hispanic, 12 percent Anglo, and 3 percent Asian, African American, or Native American. Free and reduced-cast lunch is received by 93 percent.

I. Goals:

A. **Overarching Goal:** (*What kinds of people do you want your students to be?*)
Students will be confident in their ability to apply math to other areas of the curriculum.

B. **Content Goal:** (*What kinds of mathematicians do you want your students to be?*) Students will be able to solve equations using a concrete idea.

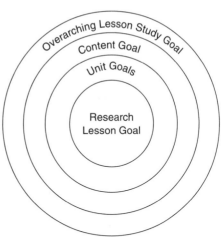

C. **Unit Goals:** (*What are your math goals for your students as a result of doing this unit?*) Orders of operations, combining like terms, and discovering multiple ways to solve problems are just a few of the concepts students will be learning in this lesson. Eighth grade is the grade level at which we need our students to practice algebraic thinking.

D. **Research Lesson Goal:** (*How does this research lesson fit with the other goals? What do you want to learn about your students from this research lesson?*) We want to see if using a restaurant and its menu is a concrete idea that can help students connect to the abstractions of variables and solving problems.

II. Description of Unit: (1 to 2 sentences)

A. How does this lesson fit into the unit?

- **Previously learned concepts:**
  Students will need to know basic operations, including addition, subtraction, multiplication, and division, as well as reading, writing, and sequences of events.

(Continued)

Figure 1 (Continued)

> They will need to have some experience with order of operations, distributive property, grouping, simplifying, solving for unknowns, multiplying decimals, formulas, and variables.
>
> - **Concepts to be learned in this lesson:**
>   Order of operations, combining like terms, and discovering multiple ways to solve problems are just a few of the concepts that students will be learning in this lesson. Eighth grade is the grade level at which we need our students to begin their algebraic thinking.
>
> - **Concepts to be used in future lessons:**
>   For future lessons and extensions, students will formalize the distributive property, arrive at formulas on their own, reinforce the order of operations, and continue to work with combining like terms.

Figure 2

Research Lesson From a Small Rural Community School

Grade Level: 5–6   **Date:** 2/24/03

Instructor: Judy Marrow   **# of Students:** 11

Class Time: 1:45–2:30   **Class Type (check one):**

Location: ☐ Regular ☐ SPED ☐ Bilingual/ESL ☐ Other
House Municipal Schools
309 Apple Street
House, NM 88121
Fifth- and sixth-grade classroom

Comments: *(Describe social cultural context of school)*
House is a small, rural community with low cultural diversity. There are approximately 80 students K–12.

I. Goals:

  A. Overarching Goal: (*What kinds of people do you want your students to be?*)
  Students will be confident in their ability to apply math to other areas of the curriculum.

  B. Content Goal: (*What kinds of mathematicians do you want your students to be?*) Students will be able to apply mathematics to science problems.

  C. Unit Goals: (*What are your math goals for your students as a result of doing this unit?*) Students will be able to compare large numbers in order to better understand size relationships of planets.

D. **Research Lesson Goal: (*How does this research lesson fit with the other goals? What do you want to learn about your students from this research lesson?*)** To see if students have a better understanding of large numbers by using scale models.

II. Description of Unit: (1 to 2 sentences) Students are studying space in science. In this lesson, comparing the sizes of planets will incorporate math.

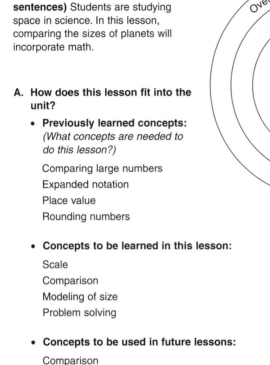

A. **How does this lesson fit into the unit?**

- **Previously learned concepts:** *(What concepts are needed to do this lesson?)*

  Comparing large numbers

  Expanded notation

  Place value

  Rounding numbers

- **Concepts to be learned in this lesson:**

  Scale

  Comparison

  Modeling of size

  Problem solving

- **Concepts to be used in future lessons:**

  Comparison

  Scale model

  Modeling of distance

Its basic design is based on the simple Japanese lesson model that asks what students are doing and what teachers are doing at each stage of the lesson. Teachers are asked to consider what students might do at different stages of the lesson and to anticipate how they might respond to student actions.

It is important to notice that underlying this rather simple template is its grounding in the problem-centered or problem-based approach of multiple, current, reform-based instructional movements and materials. The design itself expects a large amount of the lesson to involve students in solving problems and in sharing their solutions. It is not a design that fits into the traditional teacher lecture

Table 5.A   Research Lesson Plan Format—Part II

	Steps of Research Lesson	What the teacher is doing	What the student is doing	**Evaluation** *What do students need to do to be engaged in this part of the lesson?*
Launch	**Building the Context for the Lesson** *(Connecting to previous learning, meaningful contexts)*			
	Laying the Framework for Learning *(Letting students know what they will be doing)*			
Explore	**Engaging Students With the Concepts** *(Exploring, investigating, problem solving)*			
Share	**Sharing Ideas/ Solution** *(whole group, small group, writing, and presenting)*			
Summarize	**Closure** *(Connecting ideas, making sure students got content concepts)*			

model for teaching mathematics in the United States. The traditional teaching of mathematics is often described as follows:

- The teacher takes a role and goes over the homework.
- The teacher then introduces a new concept by lecturing on this concept.
- Next, homework is assigned for working on problems that provide practice with the concept.
- The teacher moves around the room or sits at the desk at the front of the room and helps students individually with their homework.

The template for the research lesson we have been using would not accommodate this type of traditional mathematics instruction. The research lesson template requires teachers to design for part of the mathematics period a time in which students grapple with problems, often in groups, and then suggest alternative solutions to problems presented by the teacher. This does not mean that the teacher sits back as the students work—instead the teacher needs to develop new skills in designing good problems leading to the desired learning, asking good questions, facilitating group discussions, and suggesting alternatives to groups who might be stuck on some part of the problem.

This will become clearer as we present the research lesson template and share some examples from real lessons. The lesson design template is basically made up of a *launch*, an *exploration and sharing*, and a *closure* in which the teacher needs to help the students make connections between all the ideas shared by students as a result of their explorations. In reform-oriented language arts classrooms in the United States, such a lesson design is often referred to as a process of getting students *into*, *through*, and *beyond* the concept to be taught. The *launch* is designed to hook the students into the lesson, while also connecting them to what was learned before. *Exploration* provides time for students to construct their own understanding of how to solve the problem that was presented in the launch. *Sharing* is an essential element that allows students to communicate their different solutions, evaluate the solutions, and move toward a deeper understanding of the concept or concepts taught. The *closure* ensures that the students have learned the concept and are ready to move on to new concepts or extend this learning into a variety of different applications.

Anticipating Student Understandings

As the teachers discuss and plan the research lesson, they need to work through each of the steps of the proposed lesson and at each step anticipate what students might think or do, what misconceptions they might have, as well as what kinds of ideas or questions the students might raise. Also, the team should try to anticipate what reactions, questions, or strategies the students might use during the lesson. Based on these anticipations, they construct the lesson to address these responses, questions, and/or strategies.

Designing the Research Lesson

Table 5.A shows the form that we have used with teachers to help them design the research lesson. The following are the key components of a carefully designed and planned research lesson. Our design provides for five steps organized within a three-part framework:

1. The launch
   - Building a context for the lesson. Some teachers have come to call this the "hook." How do you get students to want to do the problem solving that will be required in the upcoming lesson? How does this new lesson relate to what they have previously learned, and how does the lesson relate to problems they have encountered in real life?
   - Laying the framework for the learning experience. During this part of the lesson, the teacher must explain to the students what they will be doing in the lesson, how they will be doing it, and what kinds of answers the teachers might want from them.

2. Exploration and discussion
   - Engaging students with concepts
   - Sharing ideas and solutions

3. Closure and summarizing
   - Plan for closure

Comparison of This Design With the Traditional Japanese Lesson Design

We began our work by using a more traditional Japanese research lesson design. The steps are very similar but are more specifically focused on the idea of the problem. The traditional phases of the design are: (1) grasping the problem setting; (2) presentation of the problem format; (3) solving the main problem; (4) polishing and reporting solutions; and (5) summarizing and announcing the next lesson. However, some of the teachers with whom we worked had trouble with the terminology. They did not understand what it means to grasp the problem or present the problem format, so we began using terms that felt more familiar to them. Still, the underlying meaning in both models is the same. Let's look at an actual research lesson and see how each of these elements was addressed. Table 5.B shows actual lessons done by teachers in our state.

Planning the Research Lesson

In a safe environment that promotes discussion, the lesson study group teachers must share their ideas; find solutions to writing a research lesson that will engage the students with the defined concepts; and write a good research lesson that includes both the goals determined by the team of teachers and the goals set for the school, district, and state. At the beginning of the lesson study process, it is very helpful to have some *knowledgeable others* available. This is a term that might refer to instructional coaches, university faculty, principals serving as instructional leaders, outside consultants, or teachers who have experienced and worked with lesson study for at least a year or two.

We often found that the teachers, at first, were not comfortable with the sharing aspects of lesson study because they were so accustomed to being in their own classrooms and in an institutional structure that did not promote collaboration. However, in spite of their initial hesitation, eventually the teachers enjoyed the camaraderie of working together, and often mentioned that they couldn't leave their present schools because they needed to remain with their lesson study teams. Ultimately, experienced lesson study teachers will find ways to collaborate in their professional work. Our teachers have stated that this collaboration:

- Brings new ideas into their classrooms.
- Validates what they are doing in their classrooms.
- Produces better lessons with more "meat."
- Promotes close ties with the goals of the school and district and makes the lesson even more important.
- Gives them a more global view rather than just the narrow view of learning in their classrooms.
- Makes each participant look at student learning in a different way.
- Promotes a relaxed atmosphere that allows the teachers to focus on the students and the lessons that will help the students the most.

(Text continues on page 101)

Table 5.B   A Research Lesson Plan Format—Part II Variables in Algebra

What do we want to learn from this lesson?

	Steps of the research lesson	What the teacher is doing	What the student is doing	Evaluation *What do students need to do to be engaged in this part of the lesson?*
Launch	**Building the Context for the Lesson** (*Connecting to previous learning, meaningful contexts*)	–Setting the stage of using the restaurant connection.	–Students will be sitting in their seats and with their group members.	–Students need to know basic operations, including addition, subtraction, multiplication, and division, as well as reading, writing, and sequence of events. They will need to have some experience with order of operation, distributive property, grouping, simplifying, solving for unknowns, multiplying decimals, formulas, and variables.
		Possible Responses or Questions to Pose: –Have you ever eaten in a restaurant?	Possible Questions or Misconceptions: –I just tell them my order; I don't look at the bill.	
	Laying the Framework for Learning (*Letting students know what they will be doing*)	–Putting a copy of the bill on the overhead. –Telling the students about a visit to a restaurant and receiving a bill with letters and a total. Explaining that	–Listening to the scenario about being at a restaurant. –Students looking at the bill on the overhead.	–Students need to be looking at the problem presented to get them hooked into the lesson and see what they will be doing.

Steps of the research lesson	What the teacher is doing	What the student is doing	Evaluation *What do students need to do to be engaged in this part of the lesson?*
	there were all these numbers and letters on the bill. Trying to figure out how much each person owed for their portion of the food. –Asking students what they order when they go to a burger restaurant. –Choosing students to share on the board.	–Students are writing down what their order would be.	
	Possible Responses or Questions to Pose: –Why did you multiply before you added? –Why did you assign names to variables? –Why did you solve it that way? –Did someone get a different answer?	Possible Questions or Misconceptions: –I don't look at the bill. –What types of restaurants use a bill?	

(Continued)

Table 5.B (Continued)

	Steps of the research lesson	What the teacher is doing	What the student is doing	Evaluation *What do students need to do to be engaged in this part of the lesson?*
Explore	**Engaging Students With the Concepts** (*Exploring, investigating, problem solving*)	–Leading the class in the solving of the first problem. –Uncovering the rest of the problems to solve. –Handing out to groups the sheet with the monologue of orders on it.	–Trying to solve the first sample problem, then trying to solve the whole problem. –Solving the remainder of the problems on the overhead. –Putting answers on the board. –Writing problem in words. –Substituting in value and solve. –Simplifying the orders given to the cook.	–Students need to be following the teacher. –Students and groups need to follow each step or part of the lesson. –Students need to take turns and discuss the different possibilities. –Students need to record all answers to help reinforce learning of concepts. –Students need to know what they will present to the rest of the class.
		Possible Responses or Questions to Pose: –Ask the students to show the steps used to solve this problem. –What are some different ways students solved the problem?	Possible Questions or Misconceptions: –I don't get it. –What are we doing? –Does it matter what letter we choose?	–Students need to translate to other students. (Students need to have an understanding of the concept in order to translate to other students)

98

	Steps of the research lesson	What the teacher is doing	What the student is doing	Evaluation *What do students need to do to be engaged in this part of the lesson?*
Explore		The teacher, while circulating around the classroom, can ask people in groups: –Why did you multiply before you added? –Why did you assign names to variables? –Why did you solve it that way? –What operation would you use when you see "7*t*"? –Is there another way to write this equation?	–How do I know how to simplify them? –How do I know when to add and when to multiply?	
Share	**Sharing Ideas/ Solutions** (*Whole group, small group, writing and presenting*)	–Facilitating the sharing of answers to questions. Possible Responses or Questions to Pose: These questions can be posed to the groups presenting solutions.	–Working in their groups and solving the problems presented to the group. Possible Questions or Misconceptions: –What did they do? –Who has the right answers? –Am I right?	–Students need to have their answers recorded clearly on the paper. –All members of the group need to participate.

(Continued)

Table 5.B (Continued)

	Steps of the research lesson	What the teacher is doing	What the student is doing	Evaluation *What do students need to do to be engaged in this part of the lesson?*
		–Why did you write your order this way? –Did somebody get a different way? –Are they right or wrong with their answer? –Why are the poster boards of the same question the same or different?	–Why did you pick that letter?	
Summarize	**Closure** (*Connecting ideas, making sure students got content concepts*)	–Teacher will hand out the original bill to be solved.	–Students will try to solve the original bill and how much each person owes.	–Students work with the original bill and try to figure out what each person owes on the bill.
		Possible Response or Question to Pose: –What do you think is the best way to solve this problem? Why?	Possible Questions or Misconceptions: I still don't get what letter to use . . . how do you know if you should use an "h" or an "i" or a "j"?	

Laying a Framework for the Learning Experience

It is imperative that the research lesson is planned with consideration given to what concepts the students have learned; what they are doing in all of the team's curricular areas; and what the educational goals are for the students. If the students are not ready for the research lesson that the team wants to plan, what must be done to get them ready? How will the lesson integrate within the area of study or other subjects? How does it relate to what the students have learned? How does it relate to the future goals of the teacher, the school, and the district? Is it relevant and engaging? Does it promote the construction of knowledge rather than the passive memorization of facts?

Engaging the Students With Concepts

Earlier in this chapter we introduced an inquiry, constructivist approach to learning. The lesson study team must plan for how they will engage the students with the concept to be learned, all the way from the launch to the closure of the lesson. The research lesson must include sound pedagogical strategies that promote cooperative learning—connecting the concept to be learned with the world beyond the classroom walls—and the lesson must be relevant and interesting. Basic concepts may be the objectives of the research lessons, but the way the students learn those concepts must be engaging and interactive.

Closure and Summarizing

As the research lesson is written, closure is an important consideration. The lesson must be reviewed by each member from beginning to end, both individually and together. It is very helpful for the members of the lesson study team to actually do the lesson and perhaps take turns playing the roles of students and teacher. They should also review the lesson as a whole and answer the following questions:

- Are they addressing the overarching goal of the school, the goals of the subject area, or the goals of that particular grade level?
- Is the lesson engaging?
- Is the lesson relevant for the student population to whom it is being taught?

In this section of the development of the research lesson, the teachers must decide on which teacher will teach the lesson; the time of the lesson; the observers who can be there for the lesson; materials needed for the lesson; and any other miscellaneous information that is needed in order to teach this newly developed research lesson. Prior to teaching the lesson, the team should also think about what they want observers to do and how to get good, useful information from the observers.

Developing an Observation Guide

The data that observers collect is an integral part of the research lesson process and should be driven by what it is that the research group wants to know. It should be tied to their long-term goals for students, as well as to their specific research lesson goals. As always, the emphasis is on student learning, not how well the teacher is facilitating the lesson.

We have employed a number of different observers. The team of observers may include:

1. The other members of the team who developed the research lesson may join the observer team. The school must provide coverage for the observers' classes, or they may observe during their planning periods.

2. Preservice teachers from college methods classes have been encouraged to join with the lesson study process as observers.

3. Members of other lesson study teams from different schools and/or different grade levels can make good observers.

4. Administrators from the same school, another school, and the central office can make excellent observers, because they actually experience the lesson study process, and in our experience have become our best advocates for this form of professional development. Administrators who have been involved in lesson study have been the catalyst in finding funding the support time for teachers to plan, observe, and debrief the lesson.

Formal Procedures to Be Used for Observation

Prior to the observation, each observer should read through the lesson plan developed by the research group. If you have a central Web site where the lesson can be posted, this will make the process much easier, especially if you are using observers who are traveling from some distance away. The observers should make notes of the focus of the lesson and the sequence of activities the teacher and students will be engaged in during the lesson. They could participate in a Web chat or a conference phone call prior to observing the research lesson. This will ensure that the observers have a clear understanding of what they are expected to observe, and how and why they are being asked to make the kinds of focused observations they are assigned.

Observers should not interfere with the process of the lesson. This is probably one of the hardest things for observers to learn to do. As teachers and administrators, they are accustomed to helping students, and they want to step in and assist them. However, if this happens the lesson study team can't really learn what aspects of the lesson they've design helped learning and what didn't. The students and the observers will need to understand the new culture of observation of a research lesson. Observers should not help students with the problem or give them clarifying instructions. The observers should be invisible! The lesson should flow as if the observers were not present in the room. Observers will need not only directions but also guided practice in how to observe.

Catherine Lewis has suggested that there are often research goals pertaining to academic/intellectual understanding, to students' motivation, and/or to students' social behavior during the lesson. The key is that the focus should be driven by what the research group wants to know and by what constitutes good data for answering their questions. With this focus, there will be lots of specific evidence that can be discussed in relation to how well the research lesson met the goals.

There may be only one research focus during the research lesson, or there may be more than one. For instance, if teachers have a goal of having students actively engaged in their own learning and they design a research lesson that they hope will meet this goal, they should discuss what constitutes evidence of engagement. They might look for verbal, tactile, and kinesthetic evidence. Other examples of data that are to be collected could be:

- Are students participating by discussing and answering questions?
- Are students actively problem solving, writing down ideas and solutions?
- Are students leaning forward and bright-eyed?

There may be one main goal and each observer may want to focus on a group of students and gather evidence about them. One observer may want to write down numbers of students from the class who participate. The teachers may be interested in a close look at what one student does during the lesson. Maybe there are other things the research group wants to investigate. One observer may focus on engagement and another might focus on understanding.

The bottom line is that the data to be collected should be driven by what it is that the research team wants to know. During the planning stage, before the facilitation of the research lesson, there should be explicit discussion of what kinds of data will help the research team gather evidence regarding what they hope to accomplish from their research lesson. These goals must be communicated as specific data that observers should look for and document.

A final observation example comes from our 2002 summer conference. Our core teachers collaboratively discussed observation criteria related to the main topics of academics, motivation, social behavior, and student attitudes for the "cube lesson." As part of the whole-group lesson at the summer institute on lesson study, the experienced lesson study teachers served as observers. They used the following questions to guide their observations:

Academic

Are they using the vocabulary correctly?

Is there good understanding of the math content? (Are they actively demonstrating and explaining within their group? How? What are they saying and doing?)

Motivation

How many times are their hands raised?

Are they asking questions of each other?

Are they asking questions of the teacher?

Are they answering questions?

What types of body language do you observe? (shining eyes, "aha!" comments)

Social Behavior

What is the frequency of interaction? (How frequently do students refer to and build on classmates' comments?)

Is everyone valuing peer input? (How or how not?)

Are students friendly and respectful?

Is everyone participating?

Student Attitudes Toward Lesson

What did they like most about the lesson? Why?

What did they like least about the lesson? Why?

Different groups observed each of these behavioral aspects of the lessons, came together and reflected collaboratively on their observations, and then shared what they had seen with the larger group of 100 or so teachers at the conference.

Videotaping the Research Lesson

When possible, videotaping lessons is especially useful for reflecting on and refining them. As observers, we have watched a lesson—even after being involved in the planning stages—and still discovered a lot of new information through watching the video. It might also be helpful to watch some videotaped examples of lesson study to emphasize the role of observers. The videotaped lesson is valuable for both the debriefing session and the redesign of the lesson. The team of observers can go to a specific point in the lesson and document their observations. Also, the teacher who taught the lesson has a chance to sit back and view the engagement of the students and the learning process within the classroom. When teachers are teaching they don't have the opportunity to check out what all their students are doing or thinking.

One example from a videotaped lesson demonstrates this point. The teacher had asked the students to use a computer program she had designed to work on a problem involving algebra and algebra tiles. One group at the back of the room had gone far beyond what the teacher had designed and were creating some new problems on the computer. The teacher, who was fairly new, went to the back of the room and told the students to get back on the program. She didn't discover until later that they had already completed the lesson and were extending their learning.

We have asked graduate students from the university, technology coordinators from the school district, and even older students who are studying technology in their classes to videotape lessons. We started with very simple equipment and have graduated to more advanced technology that includes lapel microphones, boom microphones, and advanced videotape machines. A district could easily be highly successful with lesson study with very simple equipment, though!

Debriefing

In order to complete the research lesson cycle, all observers should commit to participating in the debriefing session. During this session the person teaching the lesson is asked to go first and express his or her feelings about what happened. Second, the lesson study team who planned the lesson should talk. This format allows the teachers to share insights about what was being studied, what worked, what did not work, and what they would change about the lesson.

After this, the observers, coaches, and others should offer their reflections on the lesson. It is important to plan at least an hour—longer if possible—for the debriefing session. Input from the observers is very helpful to the team, especially if it is well organized. All observers should plan to participate in the debriefing session and be able to provide a neat, organized, detailed summary of the data that they have collected. This data and the conversation that surrounds the observers' data will help the research lesson team to reflect upon, revise, and summarize what they have learned. Some questions to think about for the debrief include the following:

1. What parts of the lesson design helped to achieve the lesson goals?

2. What examples of student responses and reactions show how they were engaged in the lesson?

3. What could be added or changed in the lesson to better achieve lesson goals?

4. How would you expect students to respond to these changes?

The discussion during this debriefing session should focus on how well the planned activities (i.e., introduction, launch, student exploration, and so on) helped students to learn the research lesson goal. The research lesson plan itself can be used as a lens for observation and debriefing. If the feedback session follows the second implementation of the study lesson, the planning members should clarify what they tried to achieve in the lesson, and how these goals were related to the changes made between the two lessons. Teams have often decided to teach the same lesson a third or fourth time, perhaps during the next round of lesson study, because of their desire to improve the design and the learning. In some cases, teachers have also designed whole units with multiple lessons around them once they discovered what concepts the students were missing that prevented them from meeting the lesson's goals.

The Redesign of the Research Lesson

After the research lesson has been taught and the debriefing has been completed, the team who wrote the first research lesson should convene and rewrite the research lesson with all the recommendations from the debriefing session incorporated. The team must decide how the lesson should be changed, based on recommendations from the debriefing session, their reflections from watching the video, and spending some time thinking about the lesson. They will then perform the normal "bookkeeping" functions, such as who will teach the next lesson, when it will be taught, who the observers will be, and how to request support for substitutes so that they can all observe the redesigned lesson and the resultant student learning.

Conclusion

The research lesson is the heart of the lesson study process. The design, teaching, observation, debriefing, and revision of the research lesson help the teachers to focus on what the students are doing and learning as a result of their teaching in a classroom. Once teachers have participated in lesson study for several sessions, they recognize how much they have learned and enjoyed this opportunity to collaborate with other teachers. Some teachers have told us that they could never teach again in a school without lesson study. One teacher who moved to a new district has worked to convert her new colleagues to try lesson study.

Finally, the process of doing lesson study and designing, observing, and redefining several lessons are not, by themselves, enough incentive to invest in lesson study as a form of professional development. What happens is that what teachers learn as they work together to design these lessons carries over into the design of other lessons and results in changes in how teachers teach. Sometimes these changes are profound. We still work with a teacher who, prior to lesson study, provided a traditional math lesson with lecture, review of homework, and so on. Her students sat in rows and did not interact or discuss mathematics. She volunteered to teach one of the earliest lessons in her school. In order to conduct the lesson, she moved the students into small groups. Over the last few years, every time we've visited her classroom the students are still in small groups. This process worked for her in increasing student learning and problem solving.

One of the authors who directed the original MathStar project watched around 40 hours of videotape at the conclusion of the first year. What emerged were teacher behaviors that went far beyond the design and implementation of a single research lesson. Several trends emerged. First of all, the teachers began to focus on student learning, changing their attention from what they were teaching to what the students were learning. Second, they learned to answer student questions with other questions and not to jump in right away and answer the students' questions before the students had a chance to do some of their own work on answering the question. Third, they spent more time talking together about instruction and student learning and enjoying this new aspect of their professional lives. Chapter 6 discusses the final report. Each lesson study group will complete a final report that integrates what they have learned about their teaching and about their students' learning.

Extended Learning Questions

1. After answering the questions in this chapter for yourself, write a proposal to present to your lesson study team on how you would like to share what you have learned from lesson study.

2. If you haven't already done so, start an ongoing personal journal that supports continuous reflection on your thoughts and feelings as a result of participating in this new kind of professional development. Use your journal as a safe place to share the frustrations that you will naturally experience when engaging in an unfamiliar practice.

3. Consider publishing your lesson study work. Investigate the professional development magazines and journals available in your field, as well as national Web sites focused on either lesson study or teacher practice. You might want to write a short summary of an article you plan to write and submit your ideas to the editors for consideration.

4. Set up a meeting with your principal or with a district professional development administrator to share what you have been doing and suggest ways that lesson study professional development might be helpful to other teachers.

5. Consider using your lesson study work as the major component of your professional teaching portfolio. Lesson study fits well with the requirements for professional development plans and dossiers, which are required now in many states before teachers can qualify for higher salaries. Lesson study focuses on the impact on student learning of what you do as a teacher, supports gathering data, and allows you to make research-based decisions, all of which are recommended in most teacher evaluation processes.

6

Reflecting on and Sharing Your Research Lesson

With Jeff Hovermill Samatha

The sharing of the research lesson is a time for learning and for celebration. The process that a lesson study team follows to synthesize and communicate the lessons they learn during the planning, implementation, observation, reflection, and revision stages provides rich opportunities for teacher reflection on their practice. Sharing the lesson forces the research team to reflect on what they learned from the process. This chapter provides a guide for the lesson study report that will help research team members to think about what they learned about their students, themselves, and their practice.

The metacognitive step of reflecting on one's own learning is a powerful component of the overall professional development that occurs for teachers who engage in the lesson study process. During this phase, teachers consolidate the learning that occurred during earlier stages and take the professional step of organizing this learning in such a way that it can be shared with other members of the education community. This sharing may take the form of demonstration lessons, professional presentations, and/or written research reports. Teachers also gain as professionals, because like other professionals, such as doctors and lawyers, what they learn can contribute to their field. A teacher who has participated in this process remarks:

> To me, the chance for us to reflect on our learning, and to explain that learning to an audience, mirrors what we ask children to do after they have worked through a problem. Just as we require them to reflect, analyze their thought processes, and to explain their learning [lesson study sharing], requires us to do the same.

Congratulations! If you have made it to this point in the book, you have successfully planned, facilitated, and improved the organization and facilitation of a research lesson. This has taken a lot of time and effort, and has hopefully been a worthwhile endeavor. Stigler and Hiebert (2000) emphasize how crucial it is to the improvement of education that teachers build a system that provides them with a means to learn from their own experiences. Lesson study is such a means. However, as part of this system it is essential that the knowledge accumulated during your research lesson is documented and disseminated. Learning is consolidated for the teacher teams and the broader professional education community when details of the context, rationale, modifications, and findings that surround the research lesson are shared.

Education researchers emphasize that analysis of teaching that underlines the contexts and meanings associated with instructional actions makes important contributions to education research and pedagogy (Schoenfeld, 1999; Lampert, 1998). In order for this to happen, it is important for your team to reflect on exactly what you have done and learned, and to record and share this information.

Reflecting on What You Have Learned

The interactions among content, student, and teacher, as they exist within the surrounding educational contexts, have been documented as an instructional triangle (National Research Council, 2001a). During the lesson study process, your team has been able to research each of these areas of interaction:

- What is the teacher doing?
- What is the learner doing?
- How does their interaction support the learning of content?

As you plan your report, it might be helpful to organize and include the data that your team gathered during your research lesson as evidence to support the answers to each of these questions.

The Role of Content Understanding in Lesson Study

In many teacher preparation programs, teachers have not always had enough opportunity to learn about the content they teach. As we discussed in earlier chapters, there is the potential for lesson study to build in teachers a deeper understanding of the content in order for them to improve their teaching. This is why it is often useful to have a content specialist on the lesson study team or available to it as a consultant. This might involve a content professor from a nearby university, or a district-level content leader. This learning may entail building a stronger understanding of connections between procedural and conceptual knowledge within a content discipline, as well as the connection of that discipline to real-world applications and to other disciplines. An emerging concept that has grown as a result of the study of teacher pedagogy and student content learning is referred to as teacher pedagogical content knowledge (Shulman, 1987). This is a unique aspect of teaching that involves more than knowing the content. Though different from knowing the content or knowing how to teach, it combines these two abilities in a unique way. All disciplines have specific content that requires specific ways of teaching in relationship to the content. Deborah Ball and other researchers at the University of Michigan's Center for Teaching Mathematics have designed a survey of teacher pedagogical content that we have used in our own research. The survey provides some evidence that high teacher pedagogical content knowledge contributes to high student achievement. In other words, a teacher can know the content well, but not know how to teach it, or the teacher may know great teaching strategies but not possess enough knowledge of the content to help the students learn.

This is an important point, because if teachers do not feel confident and fluent with the content they are teaching they tend to just follow the textbook and engage in a teacher-directed model only. Jim Milgrem, a famous mathematician and mathematics educator at Stanford, and Karin Wiburg—who are at somewhat opposite ends of the math wars—agree that teachers cannot support students in inquiry learning of the subject if they don't know a lot about the subject themselves. In other words, if teachers know very little about mathematics they may not be able to do meaningful lesson study in this content area. In lesson study, the goal is to encourage students to do most of the learning, which then leads them to deeper and longer-lasting understanding. However, the teacher must know enough about the subject to answer the students' questions and lead them through a discovery model of questioning to move toward solutions to problems.

For the teacher, an essential basis for pedagogical content knowledge is having robust content knowledge. This deep knowledge is intimately connected to a teacher's ability to help students develop enduring understandings (Wiggins & McTighe, 1998). The National Research Council (2001a, p. 378) explains that "Teachers are unlikely to be able to provide adequate explanation of concepts they do not understand "and that ". . . not surprisingly, these teachers [with weak conceptual knowledge of mathematics] gave students little assistance in developing an understanding of what they were doing. This doesn't mean that a teacher lacking content knowledge cannot begin to learn more content through the practice of engaging in lesson study.

Within the lesson study group, there will be some teachers who are stronger in content and can help others. As in any team, there may be teachers who are stronger in instructional strategies and they too will help to design a better research lesson.

Here are some questions you might ask as your prepare your report on what the teachers did.

1. How did you ensure that you held robust understandings regarding the content and pedagogical content knowledge related to your research lesson? What resources and experiences did you draw from?

2. What did you learn about content as a result of engaging in lesson study?

The following are reflections from teachers on how they developed content for their own lesson studies.

One of the key aspects of lesson study was the opportunity for us to discuss the key mathematical concepts to be developed with learners. Far too often we as educators design our lessons based on what was presented in the text. Instead, we were able to look at data to determine areas that our students were struggling with and then research and discuss . . . the prior knowledge necessary for deep understanding. (DC)

To fully grasp the content, our team filled out a mathematical map influenced by Liping Ma (1999). Before this I never stopped to consider how powerful the Pythagorean theorem is; it is the backing behind many geometry and algebra concepts. (AA)

One of the most significant things I learned was in the area of content. It was nice to share the different ways we, as teachers, approach the content. Being able to view and discussion these different approaches helped me to expand my knowledge. (MM)

When we look back on our own mathematics learning as students, we feel that our knowledge was often superficial. Having read *The Teaching Gap* (1999) and participated in lesson study, we realize that we are deepening our understanding of what math is all about. We realize that we can help our students learn the concepts of mathematics that we ourselves were never specifically encouraged to learn. (MM)

Content and Students

Lesson study also affords multiple opportunities to learn about the relationships between students and content. You have generated key overarching, subject, and content level goals that you would like your students to be able to achieve. As a result, you are planning learning opportunities and increased access for your students to develop these content and process understandings. You are discovering, through your research, factors that support or inhibit students from being able to meet your content learning goal. In your report, you will want to communicate what you learned about student understanding.

In a day and age when teachers are required to cover such a plethora of topics and performance objectives, it is very important to communicate what you consider to be key understandings worth developing and researching and why you chose one of these key topics for your research lesson. Here are some questions to help you think about this.

1. What did you identify as overarching, subject, and content level student learning goals?

2. Why do you feel that these are essential, enduring understandings that your students need?

3. What resources and experiences did you draw from to develop these goals?

It is important to hold high expectations that all students can develop essential content and process understandings (Wiggins & McTighe, 1998). For students to meet this goal, however, they must be provided with rich opportunities to test and build on their developing understandings (Black & William, 1998). Undoubtedly, your research lesson went through growth and improvement over time, as you talked about what students were learning well and what they were having trouble learning. In order for others to learn about standards-based practices that support student development, you can use the following questions as you develop your report:

1. What assumptions did your team make about students' understandings prior to developing your research lesson? What did you feel that students would need to be able to know and do before they could successfully engage in your research lesson?

2. In what ways did your team design opportunities for students to extend their content and process understandings during your first research lesson? How did this lesson change as a result of what you learned by teaching and observing?

3. What resources and experiences did your team utilize to provide learning opportunities, and why did you decide upon using the ones that you did? Did you change resources as you continued to develop your lesson?

In order to learn from a research lesson, it is important for team members to not only observe but also to gather data. A team can decide to gather data in many different ways. Sometimes each teacher might focus on one of several groups and how they are working on a problem. Sometimes team members might be asked to look at one of a variety of factors that influence learning, such as how engaged students were with the content, how they worked together, what kinds of questions they asked, which students seemed to be having trouble, and what they noticed about these students. The important point is that gathering and using data are essential parts of lesson study that can guide practice. Understanding and using data to improve both learning and school operations is a growing movement that is supported by the lesson study process. Below are some questions your team might answer about how they gathered data.

1. What specific evidence did your team gather in order to assess whether students had met your content and process goals? How could this data be used to help answer your specific research questions?

2. What did you learn about student learning based on the data that you gathered during your research lesson? What

misconceptions did you discover that some of your students held? What are some specific examples that you can share that demonstrate what you learned about what your students understand or don't understand?

3. What modifications did your team make to your research lesson based on the data you collected and analyzed in order to better help students develop the desired understandings?

Below are some examples of teachers' comments as they worked to prepare for their presentations.

Throughout this process, I have found myself thinking more and more about how students will be learning the concepts I am teaching, and also what they need to accomplish at each point of the lesson to be successful. This is not limited to the particular class we are doing the lesson study with, but [applies] to all the classes I am teaching. (JM)

After our first research lesson, 56 percent of our students incorrectly expressed 13 feet, 6 inches as 13.6 feet. On post-assessments after revising and facilitating our lesson with a comparable class of students, only 14 percent of students demonstrated the same misunderstanding. (JC)

Lesson study focuses on student learning. Reaching students is the most important part of any lesson, and lesson study focuses on this aspect of teaching. (AA)

I got feedback from students who said they talked about the problem all lunch hour! The students showed a real hunger to find the correct solution in as efficient time and method as possible. The fact that we covered two sections in the book with one problem was a positive reaction from the students. (FJ)

In doing lesson study, I found that students like to try to solve problems more than I thought they would. They worked diligently toward a solution using whatever method they could find, and that's good. Students do like learning. (LS)

Students and Teacher

Teachers' ability to organize and manage a community of learners in a classroom environment has been demonstrated to correlate with student engagement and understanding (National Research Council, 2001b). The National Council of Teachers of Mathematics (2000) suggests:

. . . worthwhile tasks alone are not sufficient for effective teaching. Teachers must also decide what aspects of a task to highlight, how to organize and orchestrate the work of the students, what questions to ask to challenge those with varied levels of expertise, and how to support students without taking over the process of thinking for them and thus eliminating the challenge. (p. 19)

The MathStar Research Lesson Template, introduced in Chapter 3, includes specific prompts aimed at supporting teachers in developing learning environments during their research lessons. Lesson study teams, for example, are asked to plan for and reflect on: (1) how they launch the research lesson so that students become minds-on from the beginning of the class; (2) what specific content investigations students will be engaged in; (3) what questions students may have, as well as anticipated answers teachers might provide during the lesson; and (4) how the lesson will provide opportunities for communication, collaboration, assessment, and closure. In order to be able to share what has been learned about student-teacher interactions, please reflect on the following questions as they relate to the research lesson template:

1. What did you learn about the importance of, and strategies for, launching a lesson?

2. What did you learn about supporting students' investigations?

3. What did you learn about supporting and managing student collaboration?

4. What did you learn about cultivating student-student and student-teacher communication?

5. What did you learn about assessing student understanding?

6. What did you learn about putting closure to a lesson?

Here is how a few of the teachers we have worked with answered some of these questions:

We learned that having a good launch is critical to drawing the students in and motivating them to participate in the lesson. (DJ)

We wanted to make sure in our launch that we activated their prior knowledge and to have the students anticipate or wonder what was coming. (SP)

I have had my students work in cooperative groups before, but by being able to teach this lesson twice, I saw firsthand what a difference it made when the students were given rules and responsibilities to follow while working in groups. (RS)

It is important to give children think time. Many times it is easier to give the answer. I found guiding the child to the answer with questions was more beneficial. They took ownership in their learning process. (JH)

Lesson Study Process

Another important aspect of your learning that is valuable to share is related to the lesson study process as a whole. Each time you go through the lesson study process, you will learn how to better refine your focus on teaching and learning, your data collection and analysis procedures, and your collaboration with your teammates. Before embarking on your next lesson study cycle, it is a good time to reflect on what aspects of the process worked well for you and your team, and which components can be improved upon next time. Issues to think about include:

1. How was communication and collaboration encouraged and supported in your team? What suggestions do you have for continual improvement regarding openness to suggestions and shared responsibility among all team members?

2. To what extent were lesson planning, reflection, and revision grounded in actual research data? What suggestions do you have for continual improvement regarding the use of prior research and data in these areas?

3. Personally, how did lesson study support your growth as a teacher? What suggestions do you have for ways to enhance your involvement and outcomes?

Here are reflections about the process of lesson study from teachers with whom we have worked:

Before this, I never noticed how much of a chain a lesson should be. As I look back on my old lessons, they seemed so segmented: notes, examples, practice. There was no "flow" and there was no story to follow. Instead of a learning experience, it was a routine. Because the routine is taken away from the learning, the lesson has a possibility of unpredictability.

Yet because the template is complete and well planned, the general overview of the lesson is understood before the class starts. The teacher is held more accountable for the discussion in lesson study. Questions must be answered, but more important, those questions have been *predicted*. That's the beauty of lesson study. I love it. (WB)

Lesson study allows us to refine our skills by encouraging us to build our professional knowledge. (DJ)

The process of observing how students learn and focusing on specific data to collect provided many insights for me. In the normal course of teaching, you don't get a chance to see the details of learning from that perspective. The debriefing afterward was also very powerful, as we were able to share our different observations and perspectives in a collaborative setting and focus on how to improve instruction to meet our goals. (SF)

I would recommend to anyone wanting to participate in lesson study to make sure you form a good team. That is of the utmost importance. Our team was awesome. Everyone worked hard, participated willingly and openly, and we used the strengths of all team members. One of the things I enjoyed most was the open and frank exchange of ideas. So, for future lesson study participants, I would recommend that you make sure that you are on a team with people who will take the process seriously, who will do the work required, who will show up for meetings, and who will want to do what's best for the students. (LM)

Organizing What You Have Learned

Now that you have reflected on your previous experiences, it is time to prepare the final report. Important components of organizing what you have learned include thinking about who your audience is going to be and what you would like them to learn; what kind of product of your learning would like to share—written report, oral presentation, Web site, or video; and the processes your team can utilize in order to complete your product and be ready to share it with others. This section aims to support you in completing these components.

Audience

Begin by identifying your audience and thinking about what they might need and what you want them to learn about your work. Products for sharing can include teacher-developed presentations, written reports, simulated teaching, and question-and-answer sessions, among others. Here are some questions that might be helpful in identifying the content of your presentation:

1. Is your audience already familiar with lesson study?

2. Do you want your audience to learn more about how students learn particular content and/or how to utilize a particular instructional strategy?

3. Do you want administrators to recognize the professional contributions that teachers can make by engaging in lesson study?

4. Do you want your audience to do some of the activities you did with your students?

5. Will your work be shared in a formal setting—such as at a professional conference—or in a more informal one—such as an in-school meeting?

6. How many people do you expect to share your learning product with?

Depending on your answers to these questions, one or more of the following types of learning products may be more applicable to your specific situation.

Product

Here are some more details on what form your presentation might take.

Formal Report: A formal report can provide a structured format to guide reflection and share what has been done and learned during a lesson study. Guidelines for developing a lesson study final report are included in Resource A. Reports like this can supplement a final oral presentation by telling the detailed story that accompanies the developed research lesson. This is a valuable format to use when some of the audience will not be physically present, or when information will be posted on the Internet or in a book.

Without a report, other educators would not know why certain decisions were made, if and what other considerations were made, and what learning misconceptions and accomplishments they might expect to discover if they planned a similar lesson. Reading a lesson study team's final report along with the research lesson can be especially helpful for allowing other teachers to understand if, when, why, and how they might want to adapt someone else's research lesson within a different context. A helpful sample report can be found at the James Monroe Middle School Web site http://mathstar .nmsu.edu/lesson_study/lessons_topic.htm as well as others.

PowerPoint Presentation: PowerPoint presentations allow lesson study teams to summarize some of the main points they have learned in written form and to expand on these summaries and answer questions verbally. This format lends itself to a formal or informal sharing situation where the audience is physically present and can add additional explanations as PowerPoint slides are shown. Presentations using this format can easily be given to a group of peers and colleagues within a school or at a professional education conference. In any setting, these presentations are most powerful when they include actual video examples of teaching and learning from the research lesson. A short video clip can capture the look of the learning environment during a research lesson and demonstrate particularly important teaching and learning moments. The Web site Mathnm.org contains sample PowerPoint presentation.

Demonstration Lesson: A demonstration lesson is an actual research lesson that is facilitated by a research team with their actual students while an audience observes. This format, like no other, quickly and powerfully involves the audience in learning about the lesson study process and a specific research lesson. There are, of course, many logistical hurdles in conducting a demonstration lesson, not the least of which is overcoming the teachers' and the students' nervousness at having many people watching them. However, we were surprised that after doing lesson study over time the students quickly became used to additional observers and soon ignored them. The same was true for videotaping. Acting for the video camera usually subsided within one period of videotaping. However, it is necessary to have parents' permission before videotaping in the classroom.

Other factors to consider when holding a public lesson include finding space to accommodate a whole student class as well as all the observers, obtaining permission from the students' parents for their participation in the lesson, and training audience members in what they should and should not look for and do during the research lesson. This format is not usually utilized until a team has already gained much experience and confidence in conducting lesson study. One team with whom we have worked, for example, with some nervousness, recently facilitated their first demonstration lesson after having participated in lesson study privately for the previous 4 years.

Another important result of this public lesson is increased interest by district administrators in using lesson study in additional schools as a powerful form of professional development for teachers. A profound example of a demonstration lesson can be viewed online at the Mills College Lesson Study Group Web site, www.lessonresearch.net/

Process

Teamwork is essential during the planning, implementation, observation, reflection, and revision stages of the lesson study cycle, and just as important during the sharing phase of lesson study. As mentioned earlier, it is crucial that all team members reflect on the questions introduced in this chapter prior to any final product being undertaken. Once everyone has thought about the questions, decisions can be made and roles and responsibilities can be assigned.

If a report is to be written, perhaps one team member can gather and synthesize team reflections in each given area (student learning, instructional strategies, lesson study) and create a first draft of each report section. Another member can be in charge of organizing data that will be used in the report. Team members can then make sure that everyone's perspectives have been included and sufficient data has been included to support knowledge claims.

In addition, if video is to be included in the presentation, one person may be in charge of editing the clips that will be included, while another person can take primary responsibility for putting the presentation into PowerPoint form.

Just as during the research lesson process, a "knowledgeable other" can play an important role in the sharing phase. This person or persons, familiar with the work of the lesson study team, as well as curriculum, instruction, and teacher education, can moderate the development process so that a sufficient depth of reflection is included in the final product. This facilitator (or facilitators) can hopefully assume the role of a "critical friend" (Fenstermacher, 1994). This critical friend supports lesson study participants in clearly articulating their insights into aspects of the teaching and learning processes as they strive to adapt and reflect on their practice.

Disseminating What You Have Learned

Whichever learning product your team decides to share, nothing aids a high-quality dissemination effort than preparation! Make sure that all your final written products are well edited and clear to read and understand. If you are only sharing your work only in report form for print or Web publication, you must make sure that you don't leave out any important information, since you will not be there to expand on what you shared or answer any questions the audience may have. Before submitting the final report for publication, have someone who was not part of your team read your report to ensure that it is understandable by someone who wasn't involved on your lesson study team.

Prior to any oral presentation, your team should decide which team member will share what information. You should make sure that each team member rehearses in front of the team what they will say, and that there is an opportunity for the team to provide feedback and suggestions. It is helpful to time how long each part of the presentation will take. Make sure to check all technology at the site of the presentation prior to the actual presentation.

If sharing a demonstration lesson, make sure that all members of the team are clear on their roles. Besides the normal research lesson facilitation and data collection roles, some members of the team or school should also be prepared to guide the audience on where they should be and what they should be doing. Someone should be present to organize and facilitate a post-demonstration lesson debrief and discussion in a manner that has been agreed upon by the team.

Archiving What You Have Learned

After your final report and/or presentations have been given, it is a good idea to archive these learning products. The World Wide Web offers many outlets for sharing research lessons, including (1) http://mathstar.nmsu.edu (2) http://www.lessonresearch.net/index.html (3) http://www.tc.edu/lessonstudy/ and (3) http://www.mathforum.org/ among others. These sites may be able to provide links to your final research lesson and learning product.

Content area professional journals are also natural sites to disseminate what you have learned from lesson study. Copies of your final research lessons and learning products should be made available in your school library for other teachers to access later. Your school district may wish to have a bound copy available for other schools and districts to reference as well.

By taking the professional step of sharing your learning with the broader educational community, you have participated in the professional process of building knowledge in your field. As Stigler and Hiebert (1999) state: "The star teachers of the twenty-first century will be teachers who work every day to improve teaching—not only their own but that of the whole profession" (p. 179). Due to your participating in and sharing what you have learned from lesson study, these star teachers are you!

Conclusion

This chapter provides detailed guidance and real-life examples of how teachers developed and shared their final research reports. The process of developing each stage of the final research report is described. It is important to be sure to complete this final step for several reasons. It consolidates learning for the teacher readers. It also helps teachers to feel that they can be researchers and contribute to improvements in their field. Lesson study and other Web sites as well as content area professional journals are natural places to publish your learning products. Copies of your final research lessons and learning products should be made available in your school library for other teachers to access later. Your school district may like to have a bound copy available for other schools and districts to reference as well.

Extended Learning Questions

After answering the questions in this chapter for yourself, write a proposal to present to your lesson study team on how you would like to share what you have learned from lesson study.

1. If you haven't already done so, start an ongoing personal journal that supports continuous reflection on your thoughts and feelings as a result of participating in this new kind of professional development. Use your journal as a safe place to share your frustrations, which will naturally occur when engaging in an unfamiliar practice.

2. Consider publishing your lesson study work. Investigate the professional development magazines and journals available in your field, as well as national Web sites focused on either lesson study or teacher practice. You might want to write a short summary of an article you plan to write and submit your ideas for consideration to the editors.

3. Set up a meeting with your principal or with a district professional development administrator to share what you have been doing and suggest ways that lesson study professional development might be helpful to other teachers.

4. Consider using your lesson study work as the major component of your professional teaching portfolio. Lesson study fits in well with the requirements for professional development plans and dossiers, which are required now in many states for teaching salary increases. Lesson study focuses on the impact of what you do as a teacher on student learning, supports gathering data, and allows you to make research-based decisions, all of which are recommended in most teacher evaluation processes.

7

Integrating Lesson Study With Existing School Initiatives

With Susan Bussmann and Karen Trujillo

There are risks and costs to a program of action, but they are far less than the long-range risks and costs of comfortable inaction.

—John F. Kennedy

Little wonder that educators often feel overwhelmed by the enormity of their jobs! Every year they are charged with implementing newly adopted curriculum and programs. No Child Left Behind has created additional pressures, mandating that teachers ensure the Annual Yearly Progress (AYP) of students in their schools and districts. Principals and teachers are called upon to provide evidence that they are using research-based best practices to foster students' learning, and that they are able to meet the learning needs of their increasingly diverse students. At the same time, they are expected to increase both their technology skills and the integration of technology into teaching and learning in their classrooms. And the list goes on.

Under these circumstances, doing something "additional" like lesson study can be daunting.

However, this chapter's premise is that lesson study is not an "add-on" but an integral and effective way to support increased achievement, district and school curriculum alignment, data-based decision making, and quality teaching, all active ways to address reform-based pressures. Our goal in this chapter is to suggest how teachers and administrators can use many of the aspects of lesson study to address the many educational challenges that are currently faced by our increasingly diverse schools.

In fact, according to many researchers (Cohen & Hill, 2001), educational reform has not worked—but it has also not been centered around the classroom, the learning of students in classrooms, and the kind of work teachers are expected to do in their schools. In Chapter 2 we suggested that it is important for each school or district to assess its readiness for doing lesson study. In this chapter, with the input of Susan Cepi-Bussman and Karin Trujillo, researchers and professional development specialists who work with the New Mexico Learning Collaborative, we will introduce three different ways in which lesson study can be used to improve teacher and student learning within existing school initiatives. The first option involves using lesson study as one form of professional development during a district program in which funding becomes available to support the improvement of instruction. The second option describes a school district that has already structured itself to support teacher reflection, research, and collaboration through the development of professional learning communities. However, in some cases these teacher communities lack a structure and the support necessary to use the time allocated to teacher conversation to productively improve educational practice. The third model describes the Technology for Improved Achievement Regional Educational Technology Assistance Program (TIA RETA), which has been using lesson study over the past year as a way to connect weekend teacher technology workshops with teacher-directed implementation of technology in the participating teachers' classrooms.

Model 1: Lesson Study as a Professional Development Choice

One way to introduce lesson study into a district is to provide it as one of the choices of professional development encouraged by a district. This is how it was first introduced to the Gadsden Border

District, within a districtwide initiative funded by the National Science Foundation to improve mathematics teaching and learning. The project director for this initiative, known as the Gadsden Mathematics Initiative, had been involved in developing the lesson study process as part of the MathStar project and believed teachers in the district and their students might benefit from this form of professional development. Lesson study was provided as a choice for teachers beginning in the spring of 2003, with the offering of a Saturday class that teachers could attend. The nearby university offered teachers graduate education credit for attending Saturday workshops and participating in a team-based, semester-long lesson study project. The teachers either signed up as teams or were divided into teacher teams at the first meeting. The Saturday class supported teachers in learning how to do lesson study and culminated with the team's presentation and reflections on their research lessons.

This might be the easiest way to begin to implement lesson study in a district if there is funding for professional development, which is quite common, especially in the areas of reading and mathematics. Structurally, the only required elements for lesson study are willing teachers and minimal support from the administration for release time in order to plan, teach, debrief, refine, reteach, and draft a research lesson. If possible, teachers would work together during common planning times and professional development days, but if necessary they could meet at lunch or after school, or even on weekends. It is a good idea to have a lesson study coordinator for the participating district or school in order to keep track of team activities, such as team meeting times and when lessons and debriefings will occur. This role could be filled by the instructor for a class on lesson study, by an instructional leader at the school or in the district, or by one of the teachers on each lesson study team. Even if there is a central facilitator, teachers should be encouraged to develop roles for themselves within their teams such as facilitator, recorder, materials developer, time keeper, data gatherer, videographer, and so on. The open nature of lesson study ensures that this form of professional development can be used across the curriculum and by teachers at every grade level.

This model was used during the Gadsden Mathematics Initiative (GMI) where lesson study was proposed to the teachers as a means to further investigate and implement the mathematics reform curriculum that were being adopted in grades K–8 throughout the district. Teachers were presented with the opportunity to participate in lesson study by signing up for a university class, attending four Saturday sessions on a volunteer basis, and completing one lesson study cycle including two lessons, reflection, and a presentation of what they learned. Seventy-five teachers signed up for the opportunity. The sessions were used to develop overarching goals, design research lessons, and present findings. The facilitators of these sessions were available to work with the teachers and included the GMI project director, who was in the district often enough to assist with the observation and debriefing process. Teachers were also given two other kinds of choices for professional development, one of which involved learning more about the new mathematics curriculum, and the other of which was learning to align curriculum with student learning needs.

Although this initiative was substantial and the results were positive, quite a few of the lesson study teams dissolved after the class because the district had not built lesson study into the total mathematics reform effort. However, the district is still considering moving to some form of lesson study as an ongoing professional development process. One principal became sold on the idea after seeing a video of a district teacher who had been resistant to change for many years and was, as a result of her participation in lesson study, suddenly changing her instructional practice toward more problem solving by students. This teacher had literally moved her students out of rows and placed them at small group tables where they could work together. After several years, the students continue to work in this environment.

This principal's decision resulted in the first whole-school lesson study in our state, in 2003–2004. The school also happened to be a dual-language school in which all students were learning both English and Spanish while also learning the content of the elementary school curriculum. A second school, supported by the Mathematics for All (TODOS) program—designed to improve achievement for all students, especially Latino students—became a whole-school lesson study model in 2004–2005. Both whole-school models have received some support from their local universities. As part of the student outcomes study conducted for the National Science Foundation, we compared the relationships among professional development hours, professional development types, and student achievement. Students whose teachers were involved in lesson study were more successful in learning and understanding content.

The next model in this chapter is provided to show how lesson study could be easily implemented in a district where the structure and personnel are already in place to facilitate teacher professional development communities.

Model 2: Professional Learning Communities (PLCs) and Professional Development Teachers (PDTs)

The Three Crosses Public School District has recently implemented a districtwide model of professional development. This model was developed to ensure quality delivery and implementation of new initiatives and includes numerous facets that were highlighted in Chapter 3 as part of the discussion of the need for best practices in professional development (Hassel, 2004). The initial description in this section describes the model as it currently exists. The second part of this section shows how lesson study could become an integral part of this model with very little structural alteration. The district already has in place subject matter specialists, professional development teachers, teacher professional development communities, and existing mini-conferences for sharing practices.

Subject Area Specialists

These individuals are responsible for designing the workshops and providing initial training in their content areas. The district has professional development experts in most subjects for both the secondary and elementary sections. Training is done in a workshop format, where either grade-level teachers or professional development teachers are brought together to receive information from the specialist. The grade-level teachers and/or the professional development teachers are then expected to take the information back to their schools to share with the rest of the staff. Most of the workshops are held at the beginning of the school year and during the first-semester professional development days. The professional development teachers can also work in the school to model and support teaching ideas as requested by the school.

Professional Development Teachers

These individuals are former classroom teachers, and are not necessarily subject area specialists. They have been hired as site-based professional development specialists at the majority of the schools, and every school will have a Professional Development Teacher (PDT) after 3 years. They are responsible for relaying information from the district level to the building level, by passing on the information received in centralized workshops to the teachers in their buildings. Finally, the PDTs coordinate the activities of the professional learning communities.

Professional Learning Communities

Professional learning communities (PLCs) have been established for all the teachers in the district. At the elementary level, the PLCs consist of grade-level teams, and time is allotted during the school day once a week for teachers to meet for 90 minutes. At some schools, this has been done by coordinating the out-of-class activities like library, music, and physical education. If there are three teachers on a team, then their three classes rotate between the three activities in order to allow time for the teachers to meet on a weekly basis. At the middle school, the PLCs consist of subject area teachers at different grade levels or of grade-level teams who teach content across the curriculum. A typical middle school team might consist of the seventh-grade teachers who teach mathematics, language arts, science, and social studies, and may also include special education teachers and counselors. At the high school, the professional learning communities consist of subject area teachers who are grouped based on their planning periods so that they have the capacity to meet on a weekly basis for 90 minutes. As you can see, this model allows time for teachers to meet with each other every week to discuss curriculum alignment, teaching strategies, district initiatives, and other programs.

Mini-Conference

The mini-conference that takes place in this district was established more than 10 years ago. Teachers are invited to share best practices with their colleagues during one of the spring professional development days. The day is structured so that there is a keynote speaker, two 50-minute sessions with a variety of different offerings, and a closing speech given by the superintendent.

Although this model includes aspects of effective professional development, the premise in this chapter is that lesson study might provide the additional structure necessary to make new initiatives meaningful to teachers at the classroom level. Lesson study requires accountability in implementing teachers' designs for teaching and may greatly shorten the time between the introduction of something new and its implementation in the classroom. Teachers who are currently participating in this model have been engaged in a curriculum mapping process. The teachers are given time and support, but may benefit from an explicit model for making changes in their classroom instruction after this mapping has been completed. This model lends itself to the implementation of lesson study with very little modification. The personnel and structure required for lesson study are already in place, but the roles would have to be altered slightly to ensure the effectiveness of lesson study.

How Lesson Study Can Be Implemented

In this section, we describe how lesson study could be easily implemented with a school district system that is already set up to support teacher professional development.

Subject Area Specialists

The role of the subject area specialists would remain the same. These individuals would be responsible for ensuring that the teachers have the necessary information about the content area initiative that is being implemented. They would provide training and workshops for some individual teachers and also for the PDTs at the beginning of the school year and throughout the first semester. Throughout the second semester, these individuals would then be available to meet with various lesson study teams onsite as outside content specialists.

Professional Development Teachers

During the lesson study cycle, the professional development teachers could serve as mentors for the lesson study teams. Considering the fact that a lesson study cycle does not consume an entire semester, the role of the PDTs would not change for the majority of the school year. They would still be responsible for the dissemination of information and monitoring of the implementation of content area initiatives, but lesson study could be used to facilitate the implementation process. Teachers would use the new curriculum, kit, and tool during the first semester. After this, a research topic could be identified for exploration based on what the teacher team would like to research. Once a research topic has been determined, the PDT would become a support person, someone who documents the discussions; obtains resources; supports the research lesson planning; schedules the teachings and debriefings with the administration; and collects the lesson study evaluations, final drafts, and final reports of the teams.

Professional Learning Communities

The structure of the professional learning community would not be changed drastically during the planning of the lesson or the rewriting of the lesson. During the teaching portion of the lesson, the PLCs could work together so that the use of substitutes can be minimized. For example, two lesson study presentations would take place on the same day, one in the morning and one in the afternoon, so that the substitutes could be hired for one full day for two teams.

Lesson Study Conference

In this new model, the district mini-conference would include sessions and poster presentations where teams of teachers could share what they have learned with their colleagues, and a collection of research-based lessons could be established for teachers to use to effectively implement the new curriculum, kit, or initiative.

A 2-year sample calendar is provided here to assist teachers and administrators in visualizing how lesson study can be used to roll out new initiatives while at the same time tracking the progress of programs that were introduces in previous years.

Model 3: TIA RETA: Lesson Study to Support Technology Integration

The third model is the TIA RETA program currently in place in three different school districts in our state. Funds for this project, in the amount of $140,000 per year, were obtained for 2003–2004 and 2004–2005 through a competitive Enhancing Education Through Technology (E2T2) grant. It is the intention of the program administrators to seek continued funding for the expansion of this unique program.

TIA RETA was developed to provide on-site, continuous support for teachers who are intent on enhancing their abilities to integrate technology into the classroom. Much of the remainder of this chapter will be dedicated to looking at this project in depth. Susan Cepi-Bussman is the director of the project, and Karen Trujillo served as the half-time TIA RETA coordinator for one of the three school districts. A description of the three key components of this model—the TIA RETA coordinator, technology workshops, and lesson study—is provided below. Second, there will be a discussion about the impact this project has had on the participants. Third, we will discuss some of the lessons learned during the first year of lesson study. Fourth, we will provide recommendations for successfully integrating lesson study with technology. The final

Month	Activity
August–October	Subject area specialists conduct workshops to introduce lead teachers and PDTs to new initiative, curriculum, and kit.
August–December	Introduction of initiative at the building level done by lead teachers and PDTs.
August–December	Teachers use new materials in class and record what seems to be working and what seems to be problematic.
January	PDTs introduce the use of lesson study to the teachers during PLC time using articles, videos, and books.
February	Teachers develop an overarching goal for the students at the building level and at the team level.
Late March	After testing, teachers identify an area of the new curriculum that they would like to use to develop a research lesson.
April/May	Teachers use PLC time to develop a research lesson, with guidance from the specialists and the PDT. Lesson study cycles are completed.
May	Teams share their experiences and findings informally with other teachers at the building level.
Summer	Teachers identify focus for upcoming school year, based on data about student performance.
August	Lesson Study team works with their facilitator, principal, and other members of the school improvement team to refine overarching goal for district/school/team, based on data about student performance.
September	Specialists begin providing workshops for lead teachers and PDTs in the new curriculum to be studied in late spring. PDTs and teachers initiate second lesson study cycle, focusing on the initiative from year one during PLC time.
October	PDTs and teachers use PLC time to develop research lesson and complete lesson study cycle within a 2-week period.
August to December	Teachers use materials for new initiative in class and try to identify a good research lesson topic.
November	Teams prepare for lesson study conference.

(Continued)

(Continued)

Month	Activity
December	Teachers and PDTs identify a topic for the spring research lesson.
January	Lesson study conference is given for and by teachers.
January/February	PLCs are used to reflect on good teaching practice across the curriculum.
Late March	Teachers and PDTs initiate third lesson study cycle based on the initiative from year two.
April/May	Teachers complete lesson study cycle and share findings and lessons informally at the building level.
Continuous	This model can be repeated on an annual basis with adjustments for the needs of the teachers and the introduction of new curriculums.

section of the chapter compares the monetary commitments involved in providing this and other types of support for teachers.

Components of TIA RETA

The Project Coordinator

The key component of TIA RETA is the presence of a coordinator at each site. For this project, the coordinators were required to have certain skill sets. First of all, they had to be comfortable with technology and have experience using technology in the classroom. Second, they had to be experienced classroom teachers who are used to implementing best practices in their instruction. Third, they had to be willing to share their experiences and encourage other teachers without being overbearing or directive in their approach. For TIA RETA, each coordinator serves as a part-time employee to manage workshops and lesson study cycles as well as work in participants' classrooms. In our experience, one half-time person can effectively coordinate a maximum of three lesson study teams involving 10–12 teachers. This person usually teaches in the district during the other half-time of their position. If a school or district is interested in implementing lesson study on a larger scale, this individual would have to serve in a full-time capacity, or additional personnel would be needed, depending on the number of teachers involved in the project. Either way, the coordinator has three major roles: technology workshop instructor; lesson study coordinator; and classroom mentor.

As the instructor for the technology workshops, the coordinator is responsible for assisting the teachers in determining their current skill levels with technology and helping them progress to where they can effectively integrate technology with content learning in the classroom. The workshops serve as models of how technology can be used to assist student learning, while at the same time increasing the capacity of the teachers. The group support fostered by collaborative planning in the tech workshop is further enhanced by participation in lesson study. Lesson study adds the essential step of taking what was learned in the RETA technology integration workshop and studying how well these technology-based strategies help students to learn content.

Making the lesson study process as accessible as possible for the teachers is one of the primary jobs of the coordinator. In many cases, management issues such as setting up meeting times, finding substitutes, documenting discussions, and collecting paperwork can be so overwhelming for lesson study team members that they get discouraged about participating in the process. When the teams meet, the coordinator is present to observe and document the discussion about the design of the research lesson. In some cases, the coordinator may offer suggestions, but the development of the lesson is the responsibility of the teachers. During the lesson presentations, the facilitator assists with observations and videotaping. In debriefing sessions, the coordinator is responsible for facilitating the discussion and documenting what is said so that each team member can fully focus on the lesson. The process involves calling first on the teacher who did the teaching, then the team who designed the teaching, and finally additional observers who observed the lesson and might want to contribute to the lesson.

As a classroom mentor the TR coordinator is available to model technology-enhanced lessons, co-teach, co-plan, observe, and support teachers' risk taking as teachers become more comfortable in using technology in the classroom. The coordinator's weekly presence provides teachers with the support and encouragement necessary to become comfortable with the idea of shifting from a teacher-centered classroom to a learning-centered classroom in order to more fully implement technology.

RETA Technology Workshops

The second component of the TIA RETA project includes the technology workshops using the RETA model (see http://reta.nmsu.edu), which are attended by all the participating teachers. RETA workshops are ongoing and are organized around a series of six full-day Saturday sessions provided over the course of a school year. At each of the TIA RETA sites, these sessions are used to enhance teachers' technology skills and provide technology-integrated activities. Because each site has different needs, the teachers themselves determine what information is covered in these sessions. Each RETA workshop is curriculum-focused, collaborative, real-world connected, and presentation oriented. The participants work collaboratively as "students" to complete an activity or a project that can in turn be used in the classroom. Within this framework, technology is treated as a learning tool that can support the implementation of best practices. The goal is for teachers to experience how technology can be used to implement learning-centered instructional approaches in different content areas.

There is a high degree of overlap between the RETA model and the lesson study process, in that the underlying theory of learning is constructivist. Both programs are developed so that students are helped to make meaning of the content being learned through engagement and problem solving. Essentially, both programs are aiming to help teachers shift to a more learning-centered classrooms in which an inquiry-oriented approach is guided or facilitated by the teacher. Both approaches also build collaborative professional relationships between teachers. In such learning environments, students are actively, and often collaboratively, engaged in hands-on, problem-solving activities in which they explain their thinking. The technology workshops are designed to empower teachers with the skills necessary to use technology to foster this type of a learning environment. Lesson study provides the additional structure necessary to take these skills from the Saturday workshops directly into the classroom, with the support of a lesson study team and the TIA RETA coordinator.

Lesson Study

The facilitation of lesson study in TIA RETA is the key to bringing technology integration to life in the classroom. During the conception phase of this project, Susie Bussman, the RETA coordinator, was discussing with a colleague the challenge of providing classroom-level support for teachers' integration of technology. He described his lesson study work with MathStar. Lesson study seemed like the entree into the classroom, with a direct focus on student learning and student-centered instruction. The non-content-specific framework of lesson study lent itself to technology integration, even though it had been used traditionally in this country primarily in mathematics. Bussman read *The Teaching Gap* (Stigler & Hiebert, 1999) and *Lesson Study* (Lewis, 2002), and the TIA RETA project was born.

At the beginning of the project, an overarching goal was developed by the participating teachers. This collaboratively developed goal was "Our students will be compassionate, responsible problem solvers who are respectful of themselves and others." School-teacher teams work within this goal as they develop unit plans and research lessons. Clearly, this goal is cross-curricular, which is important because each school site determined a subject area that addressed their students' learning needs based on standardized test scores and teacher observation. At the Cobre site, it was decided that the focus would be science, and this has stayed consistent through both years of the project. At Poquaque, mathematics has remained the focus area for both years project. At the Truth or Consequences site, the subject area has varied depending on the team and the cycle. Through four lesson study cycles, the subject areas covered by this group have included science, writing, presentation, social studies, and math. The table on the next page shows a synopsis of TIA RETA activities for the first 2 years.

Impact on Teachers' Instructional Practice

Throughout this book, there has been an extensive discussion about how to do lesson study, and this chapter has focused on how to integrate lesson study to strengthen professional development and school improvement for a school or district. However, the question remains: Why should we do lesson study? What can lesson study add to the previous professional development provided by RETA on technology-integrated instruction? The following section includes an in depth look at the impact TIA RETA has had on the teachers involved in the program and focuses frequently on the teachers' reflections in their own words.

Collaborative, Engaged Learners

The teachers believe that the collaborative planning designed to integrate RETA workshop lessons into the curriculum has increased the use of cooperative learning, hands-on learning, and centers. These are the words of the teachers as recorded by Bussmann.

- I just have to say this because most teachers feel like they need to be the teacher instructor leader and they want the kids to work on their own. But as teachers we've all sat here and agreed that we do better working together in coming up with ideas. And when we don't get something, somebody else does.

Time	Activity
August 2002	TIA RETA coordinators are trained in lesson study by the MathStar staff. Teachers are identified to participate in TIA RETA at the three sites.
September 2002	Teachers are introduced to lesson study during a Saturday session conducted by the MathStar staff, and the overarching goal was developed. Teachers attend first technology workshop.
October 2003	Teachers attend half-day inservice to develop research lesson.
November 2003	Teachers participate in first lesson study cycle (two half-day sessions per team). Teachers attend Saturday session to revise lesson between lesson presentations.
December 2003	Teachers attend second technology workshop.
January 2004	Teachers attend third technology workshop.
February 2004	Teachers begin to develop second research lesson.
March 2004	Teachers attend fourth technology workshop.
April 2004	Teachers attend fifth technology workshop.
April 2004	Teachers complete second lesson study cycle. The final Saturday session is used to revise lesson between presentations.
May 2004	Some teachers attend lesson study conference.
September 2004	Teachers attend technology workshop and use half-day inservices to develop third research lesson.
October 2004	Teachers go through third lesson study cycle using the Saturday between presentations to refine lesson.
November 2004	Teachers attend lesson study conference and some teams present findings. Teachers attend technology workshop.
December 2004	Teachers begin to develop research lesson for fourth cycle. Teachers attend technology workshop.
January–February 2005	Teachers go through fourth lesson study cycle.
March–May 2005	Teachers complete technology workshops and final reporting for grant cycle.

Yet we expect our kids to get it when we just stand up there and tell them, "We are going to do this." So I think that is a pretty big thing.

- Lesson study has helped me to think differently about student learning. It shows you how to become more of a facilitator with your approach to teaching.

- I have used cooperative learning more this year than I have at other times. I am still very aware of what's going on. I am circulating. But I see that my kids are really good teachers.

- Both lesson studies that we did this year focused on a lot of student-led group work. And I never really put that much emphasis on collaboration within a small group of kids. I think that giving the kids the opportunity to work together and to teach themselves was beneficial.

An Increasing Orientation
Toward Looking at Learning

Lesson study has allowed these teachers the structure to reflect more on student learning in order to improve their practice. Teachers seem more willing to facilitate learning after participating in lesson study. Catherine Lewis (2002) calls this process "developing an eye for student learning." The journal reflections and conversations from participating TIA RETA teachers document this changed perspective.

- I am more willing to turn over the reins to the students as peer teachers and facilitate their learning from the sidelines. I tended to lecture more than I needed to.

- Students helping students seems to be more effective than teachers giving lectures. The traditional lecture approach still has its place for introductory purposes, but students need time to brainstorm and interact with each other as they learn.

- With this emphasis on testing and responsibility for all these concepts . . . I've gone into more drilling and more practice sheets. And I hate it. I *hate* that! And I know my kids hate that. And when we did our lesson study there were a lot of concepts that the kids had to learn and had to focus on . . . and they still learned. So I guess my point is, I thought [about] me being up there and drilling this stuff, you know, and kind of like shoving it down their throats and making them do these worksheets . . . it isn't better teaching.

- Before, I assumed students had prior knowledge. Now, I no longer assume. A pretest and a posttest are a must. Hands-on learning is time-consuming but necessary for learning.
- Mistakes made by teachers or students bring about learning.

Increased Valuing of Technology Use in the Classroom

The process of connecting technology training workshops with lesson study has led to an increase in teachers' reflecting on the potential impact of technology in the classroom. Below are some of the comments made regarding the use of technology in the classroom:

- I learned the difference between using technology for the sake of using technology and using technology effectively. And I think that is something that I will definitely take with me next year when I start out the year.
- I've become more confident. I'm a slow learner. I take more time learning things. But I've become more confident with technology.
- I feel more comfortable using technology than I did. Just going out there and experimenting with different things. So I do feel more comfortable.
- I have started using more technology in every aspect of learning. The lessons are more creatively done and the students' interests are piqued. As a result, they get more out of the lesson.

Teachers' "Aha!" Experiences

Providing teachers with the opportunity to study how students are learning resulted in many "aha!" moments related to technology integration *and* good teaching practice. Their comments showed the insight developed as a result of integrating the two professional development approaches.

- My "aha!" moment was realizing how much the students know about computers and how much they can teach me, the grown-up. Kids are good teachers, too. They instinctively know how to break down the lesson. I had one child who taught me how to copy a picture and get it to the PowerPoint slide. She took pride in teaching me, and the other children thought it was cool.

- My "aha!" moment came when I worked with the computer teacher and she told me that my students had never gotten on the Internet in class before. Then I saw how excited they got about learning the concept of patterns using a new Web site. It was great!

- My "aha!" moment was when I realized what a useful and effective tool a PowerPoint presentation could be in the classroom. I want to try and build some of these over the summer for next year. That way I will be more comfortable with them and can have students create them next year also.

- I really learned a lot about the PowerPoint and just how to be supportive of the kids. A couple of the kids know more than I do. And I learned how to swallow my pride and learn from them. And I think that really empowered all of the kids because I heard them asking each other one day, "Now did you teach her how to do that?" [and she said] "Yeah, I did . . ."

Additional Teacher Reflections

Teachers made many interesting comments as they participated in and reflected on their participation in lesson study in the TIA RETA project. Some of these comments are included below.

- It is effective to engage students' interest at the beginning of a lesson with a "hook."
- It is important to establish a clear learning purpose and share it with students.
- A teacher must think ahead and prepare for student questions and misunderstandings.
- The quality of planning directly impacts the quality of student learning.
- Learning increases with hands-on experiences.
- Using technology motivates students.
- Working cooperatively in groups is engaging for students.
- Presenting material using technology is more interesting than the textbook.
- Matching the difficulty of activity to students' levels of independent learning is important.

Implementation Lessons Learned

The following section discusses the implementation lessons learned in the first year of the program. Some of the suggestions are related to the implementation of lesson study in general, while others are specifically about things to consider if technology is part of lesson study.

Focus on the Overarching Goal

We found that teachers had difficulty keeping the overarching goal in mind when planning lessons. We suggest making a big banner of the lesson study goal and posting it in every classroom as a daily reminder to teachers. This also helps students become aware of the goal and what is expected of them. Using the forms provided in this book that ask for a description of the four levels of goals for each research lesson should also help teachers to keep their eyes on the lesson study's overarching goal.

Less Is More

During year one of TIA RETA, the research lessons tended to be very large and instead of being a 45-minute lesson, some lessons ended up running longer than 90 minutes. Even if the school provided 90-minute blocks for lessons, the content still covered too many concepts for deep learning. Perhaps one of the most profound things we learned is that less is actually more. It is important to concentrate on keeping things simple in order to go for greater depth in the research lesson. A planning-backwards approach, with the assessment for learning built in, would help simplify the lesson so that the focus is on student learning and not on delivery. This is a common trend that we have found when introducing lesson study. At first teachers want to include everything, including the kitchen sink, in their first research lesson. Soon, teachers learned to teach fewer concepts in order to focus more on the learning opportunities that could be provided to learn a concept deeply. Sometimes teachers learned to take the overly large lesson and break it down into smaller, sequential lessons. Eventually teachers learned to pick the best research lesson in order to provide a useful window into the unit plan and the larger content and overarching goals.

Wider Perspective

Research lessons must be seen as pieces of a unit, not as the unit itself. We think that beginners tend to want to throw everything they want the students to learn into one big research lesson. It is important for teachers to focus on the main concepts to be taught in a unit, and then learn how to sequence the lessons that lead to unit understanding. In some cases, the teams chose the student project presentations using the technology as the content to be learned in the research lesson. However, any of the mini-lessons where students were learning to use PowerPoint and the Internet to show their understanding of concepts may have been far more appropriate for a research lesson than the final presentation. The final presentation did not really offer a rich opportunity to observe the teacher as facilitator or the students as problem solvers. In the debriefing discussion, the group realized that perhaps one of the lessons leading up to this culminating activity would have made a better research lesson.

Focus on Observing Students' Learning

The TIA teachers identified the opportunity to observe in each others' classrooms as a very valuable aspect of lesson study. This observation, as well as the entire lesson study process, renewed the teachers' interest in what students were learning. For many, their focus quickly shifted from what the teacher was doing to what the students were doing. This process is enhanced when the teachers carefully plan for the data collection they will do during the lesson. Because U.S. teachers are not used to just watching in the classroom, the natural urge is to help any students who are struggling. We have even seen principals rush in to help a student. Instead, everyone must understand the purpose of observation during the lesson. The teacher team and other observers should be given a form for collecting specific data. As mentioned in Chapter 4, this observation data might be divided into different parts, such as what the students are doing academically, how they are working together, and who is participating in the lesson. Then different observers can be asked to look for different kinds of behavior that can be shared during the debriefing. Sometimes the lesson involves four or five groups of students. We have found it helpful to ask each observer to focus on a specific group and then provide feedback after the lesson. Whatever the format, all issues related to observation should be discussed ahead of time so that the observers do not interfere with the lesson. Observers should also have a copy of the lesson plan several days before the lesson is taught.

A Valuable Culminating Activity
Is Important for Maximum Impact

As discussed in Chapter 5, the sharing of the research lessons and what the teacher team learned while doing lesson study is an essential part of the lesson study process. After the first lesson study cycle, the TIA teams prepared final lesson study reports, as Japanese teachers do. However, the TIA teachers thought that this final report was a waste of time that could have been better spent collaboratively planning another lesson. And to a certain extent they were right, because the project had not provided an audience for their reports other than the project director. In Japan, publishing the final lesson study report makes sense because there is a real audience for this information, and research lessons are used and often refined over several cycles, sometimes for several years.

After the second lesson study cycle, the TIA teams got together and informally shared their lessons and then worked together analyzing student work products. This was considered a meaningful culminating activity directly related to real teacher work and student learning.

In the second year of the program, TIA teachers have taken a big step professionally, with several teams presenting their lessons formally at an annual state-level conference. Participation in the conference also helps teachers to see themselves as professional researchers with much to contribute to solving educational problems, especially as they relate to classroom teaching and learning. Whatever form it takes, a culminating activity or product is an important part of the lesson study process. It brings everything together, helps strengthen shared understanding, provides closure, and contributes to a sense of achievement and celebration.

Lesson Study and Technology Integration

TIA was a unique project with many variables to address, including the use of technology integration as a central part of the lessons. To increase the likelihood of success when implementing a lesson study program with a technology integration focus, assessment of the technology infrastructure and teacher readiness in the participating schools and classrooms is recommended. With or without lesson study, the stability of the technology infrastructure and the degree of access to technology are going to impact teachers' efforts to integrate technology. For true integration to take place effectively, we recommend that the following technology infrastructure be available at the school site.

- Wireless network access.
- Classrooms with four Internet-connected computers.

- Access to a digital camera.
- Access to an LCD projector.
- A computer lab and/or a mobile laptop lab with an integrated software package, such as Microsoft Office.
- A teacher laptop, preferably wireless, with an integrated software package and Internet capabilities.
- Open lines of communication with and the support of the technology staff, especially if students and teachers are going to depend on the network for accessing the Internet and/or for storing work in progress.

Level of Experience With Technology Integration

It is also important, if technology will be a variable in the lessons, that the staff conduct an assessment of the amount and type of professional development (PD) for technology integration that teachers have already experienced. The level of technology skill and attitudes toward using technology may have an impact on the success of the lesson study. In the TIA RETA project, many of the teachers who participated in the program had already had at least a year of technology integration professional development with the RETA program. As a result, they were very familiar with a project-based curriculum approach to technology integration. In fact, many of the TIA participants who volunteered did so in large part because of their familiarity with RETA.

Another factor in relation to technology is the teachers' attitudes toward using technology for teaching and learning. In our experience, the teachers' desire to learn, openness to trying new things, and capacity for risk taking are even more important than their technology skills. Although it is helpful for participating teachers to have basic technology skills and some understanding and experience with technology integration, it is not necessary for all the teachers to be technology experts or already be integrating technology. Their attitude is what really counts, because this will be the factor that determines the level of buy-in that the teachers display throughout the program. We recommend doing a preassessment survey to determine where the teachers are in terms of their skills and their attitudes toward technology integration.

Finally, we do not recommend requiring technology integration during the first lesson study cycle for teachers new to lesson study. Depending on the level of teacher comfort using technology, and their degree of familiarity with integrating technology, it might be best not to require the use of technology during the first lesson study cycle. Of course, some groups may choose to use technology, but it should not be required.

Although increasing students' use of technology for learning was TIA's primary goal, it should be stressed that integration should occur where appropriate to support and enrich student learning, but that technology should not be used simply for its own sake. The following questions can help guide the thoughtful integration of technology:

- Who is using the technology?
- What technologies are being used?
- How is the technology being used?
- Why use this technology in this activity?
- What does using the technology allow you to do that you couldn't do with out the technology?

Categories of Teacher Technology Use

TIA RETA was designed in the belief that supporting teachers' use of technology personally and professionally would eventually lead to the integration of technology into student learning activities. Preliminary data show that TIA teachers did become more confident in their use of technology, and that they started to use technology more in the classroom and in a greater variety of ways.

The following list of stages illustrates different categories of teacher technology use, sequenced in four stages of increasing integration.

Teachers' Use of Technology

- Personal purposes—e-mail, digital photos, Palms/IPaqs, and so on.
- Professional purposes—grades, lesson planning and resources, class newsletters, presentations, and education listservs.
- In-class students' passive—presentations, data collection, digital photos, and so on.
- In-class students active—interactive learning activities.

This hierarchy of teachers' use of technology can also be seen as a sequence of growth stages in terms of their professional abilities. With all changes in instruction, it is common for teachers to have beliefs about what they would like to do before fully integrating new teaching models (Joyce & Weil, 1996). In addition, teachers—and the rest of us—are usually happiest when we can begin using an innovation in a small but personally meaningful way. After becoming personally comfortable with a tool, teachers will then consider how they might want to adapt or change their teaching. Teachers naturally begin by altering the traditional teaching method that they are used to—the presentation of information to students—and only later are they able to turn over more of the learning decisions to the students. The last two stages above are parallel to what we have observed as teachers become more confident as lesson study practitioners. In our experience, one of the hardest steps for teachers to take in the U.S. is to provide time for students to learn to answer their own questions. During the research lesson, while students are working together to solve problems, we have had teachers comment to us that they feel as if they are not really teaching. Engaging teachers in lesson study goes a long way toward helping to change this perception specifically and the culture of teaching in general.

Final Reflections on the TIA RETA Project

The integration of technology into teaching and learning was fostered by the lesson study process because it directly addressed the teachers' need to see students actually using technology effectively. Collaborative planning of the research lessons allowed teachers who had more experience integrating technology to share the "how" of integration with less experienced teachers. Designing a research lesson, observing or teaching students, deconstructing that lesson with peers, and reworking it provided a much deeper understanding of technology integration in action than had occurred prior to integrating lesson study with the technology integration workshops. The combination of experiencing lesson study, knowing they had supportive team members nearby, and access to in-class support from the facilitator helped the TIA teachers take steps to increase their use and integration of technology.

Looking at the Cost

It is important to teachers and administrators who might be interested in supporting lesson study in their schools to consider the possible costs of doing so. The following section compares the models presented in these chapters in terms of probable cost. (The sample budgets are approximations, as costs may vary in different regions and based on what districts pay.)

Budget for Model 1: Lesson Study as a Professional Development Choice

Budget

Activity	Purpose	Cost per teacher	Total Cost *10 teachers for 1 lesson study*
Saturday/ Afterschool workshops	A minimum of four 4-hour workshops needed to develop, refine, and complete research lesson	$200–$250 in stipends	$2,000
Facilitator	Facilitates workshops and assists teachers through LS cycle	$250 Saturday workshop	$1,000
Substitutes for two half days	Teaching and debriefing	Depending on district, costs $75/teacher	$750
Course credit from cooperating university		$200/three credits	$2,000
		TOTAL	**$5,750**

Advantages

The advantage of using this model is that it can be done on a small scale and can be adapted by teams or administrators to suit their individual situations. If a teacher team wants to do lesson study, it is possible even if they have very limited financial support. Such teams might choose to meet during common planning times or after school instead of in a formal workshop setting and not demand pay for workshop days. Even this cost could be minimized by using teachers' aides, other support staff, or student teachers from a nearby university's teacher education program. However, we have not heard of many lesson study groups—especially during the first few years of lesson study—who have been successful without a coordinator and some incentives for the teachers. We do know of several lesson study teams who have continued to run their own lesson study programs without financial support after 2 to 3 years of supported lesson study work. Ultimately, it might be possible to embed lesson study as the preferred method of professional development into a school or district structure, thus reducing the extra costs required.

Budget for Model 2: Professional Learning Communities and Professional Development Teachers

Budget

Activity	Purpose	Cost per teacher	Total Cost *30 teachers for one lesson study*
Professional Learning Communities	Allow time for teachers to work together within the structure of the school day	$0	$0
Professional Development Teacher	Facilitates PLC time and assists teachers through LS cycle	$0	$40,000
Substitutes for two half days	Teaching and debriefing	$75/teacher	$2,250
		TOTAL	$42,250

Advantages

The second model is probably the most structurally sound model for lesson study, for many reasons. First of all, it allows for lesson study to be done during the school day and does not require an extensive time commitment from the teachers outside of school time. Second, lesson study becomes part of the school culture, much as it is in Japan, where teachers are seen as professionals who add to the knowledge base of their profession. Third, a district could build a large body of research-based lessons developed by their own teachers that focus on student learning. Such lessons can support the implementation of districtwide curricula. Finally, this model can be used to improve teaching across the curriculum on a continual basis.

Disadvantages

Model 2 requires the support of administration at the building and district levels. It also requires that different schools agree across the district on supporting this form of professional development. This is a large-scale implementation plan that would take extensive planning in order to foster the necessary buy-in from all the affected parties, including the parents and other community stakeholders. Some teachers may not be interested in using their professional learning communities to engage in lesson study, so it is vital that there is an effort made to educate teachers about lesson study, and how it can be useful for all teachers in all subject areas and grade levels, before going forward with this plan. It might be possible to begin by using lesson study within just one subject area, such as mathematics or reading, where there is a need to change how teachers are teaching in order to improve student achievement. It is not necessary to do lesson study across the whole curriculum.

Budget for Model 3: TIA RETA Project: Integrating Lesson Study and Technology Use

Budget

Activity/Personnel	Purpose	Cost per teacher	Total Cost *(10 teachers)*
Facilitator	To teach technology workshops, facilitate lesson study activities, and mentor teachers	$2,500	$25,000
Teacher Stipends	Incentives for attending technology workshops	$100/workshop for 6 workshops $600	$6,000
Technology Incentives	To foster use of technology	$300 for handheld computers	$3,000
Substitutes	Nine half-day sessions for development of lesson, professional development and the teaching/debriefing of the research lesson	$75/day for 4.5 days totaling $337.50	$3,375
College credit	Graduate credit was offered as a reward for the intense LS experience	$150/teacher per course	$1,500
		TOTAL	$38,875

Advantages

There are numerous advantages of the TIA RETA model. First of all, this model can be centrally administered from a university or a regional center and can be implemented at multiple sites in multiple districts. Second, this model can be used specifically to support the integration of technology. It can also be used to support the implementation of other kinds of learning. Finally, this model is flexible, and costs and incentives can be adjusted to meet the needs and desires of the funding agency, the teachers, and the grant administrators.

Disadvantages

The disadvantage of this program is its sustainability. The TIA RETA project is currently grant-funded, and the teachers are continually receiving incentives to participate in this project. Without this continued funding and incentives for the participating teachers it is entirely possible that lesson study would cease to exist.

Conclusion

In this chapter, three comprehensive models of lesson study are presented. The first model can be used by any interested group of teachers willing to form a team and receive minimal support. However, additional support is recommended for the sake of sustainability. The second model demonstrates how lesson study could be used within the professional development structure of a district that already values teachers working collaboratively to improve teaching practice across the curriculum. The final model provided a description of how lesson study can be used in conjunction with technology workshops to increase the level of technology integration while at the same time affecting teaching practice.

Facilitators of the TIA RETA grant have learned a great deal about lesson study and its impact on teachers. There is ample evidence provided in their data (including observations, teacher interviews, and achievement test data) to show how lesson study has made a positive difference in the participants' instructional practices. It is our belief that lesson study is not only very cost-efficient but also serves as a value-added form of professional development, because it can deliver a lot of "bang for the buck" in terms of improving teachers' instructional practice.

Traditionally, professional development is delivered in a workshop format, in which costs can range from $500 to $5,000 per day. During these workshops, new ideas, new initiatives, and new requirements are introduced to the teachers. The challenge lies in ensuring that there is a transfer of information from the workshops into the classrooms. It is our belief that lesson study provides the necessary structure to ensure that this transfer takes place. Through lesson study, teachers receive the necessary follow-up support to change classroom practice in ways that positively influence student learning and teacher learning.

Lesson study teams can foster the formation of professional learning communities in which teachers support each other as they implement new strategies into their classroom practice. Furthermore, the framework allows teachers to investigate how students respond to new initiatives. If the point of professional development is to improve teaching and enhance student learning across the curriculum, lesson study is a very cost-effective way to achieve these goals.

Extended Learning Questions

1. Discuss the three different models for integrating lesson study into existing district or school initiatives. Which one most closely describes your own school's situation? What adjustments would need to be made if you were going to introduce lesson study?

2. Develop a proposal for introducing lesson study into your school or district. Include a rationale, an implementation plan, and a budget.

3. Think about possible other ways to introduce lesson study that have not been discussed in this chapter. Write a different model and share this with others.

Resource A

Professional Development Materials

These are additional support materials for teachers and administrators interested in implementing lesson study in their schools or districts. They have been placed here because they are not seen as an integral part of the text, and because they may be useful only to some readers. These materials are organized by chapter.

Chapter 2: Building Lesson Study Communities

Professional Development Activities

The table on the next page contains advice for introducing teachers to lesson study. Feel free to modify these exercises as dictated by your district needs.

Teacher Collaborative Study Groups

Usually when teachers read articles documenting the gaps in United States mathematics teaching and learning—and the work involved with conducting research lessons—lots of ambitions and frustrations involving our own experiences with mathematics education are triggered by the readings, examples, and discussions. Now, after having had a chance to reflect on these topics, How are you feeling about engaging in this process?

Activity 1	
Introductory Lesson Study Readings	
Purpose	The goal is to introduce some of the rationale and foundations for lesson study to teachers. These readings, Improving Mathematics Teaching and A Lesson is Like a Swiftly Flowing River, communicate some of the important aspects of lesson study from *The Teaching Gap* (1999) and *Lesson Study* (2002) without requiring that teachers read the books to get started with lesson study. Through reading and discussing these two articles, teachers should come to understand the importance of studying, and communicating about, teaching.
Materials Needed	• Improving Mathematics Teaching (http://www.ascd .org/publications/ed_lead/200402/stigler.html) • A Lesson is Like a Swiftly Flowing River (download from (download from http://www .lessonresearch.net/res.html)
Estimated Activity Time	Teachers should read these articles before they will discuss them. These articles should not take much more than an hour to read. Another hour should be allotted for discussion of the articles.
Steps for Facilitation	1. Distribute articles to participants. Let them know that these articles are condensed from *The Teaching Gap* (Stigler & Hiebert, 1999) and *Lesson Study* (Lewis, 2002). **(Presenters should have already read these books and participated in lesson study themselves!)** 2. Have them read the articles and highlight important sections. 3. Provide them with opportunity to discuss these readings. You may want them to respond in writing to some of the questions below and/or use them as small- and/or large-group discussion topics. 4. Possible discussion topics are: • Stigler and Hiebert (1999, p. 29) state that "Teaching, not teachers, is the critical factor to improving schools" since "standards and assessment, though necessary, are not enough.

Activity 1 **Introductory Lesson Study Readings**	

	Standards set the course, and assessments provide the benchmarks, but it is teaching that must be improved to push us along the path to success." Do you agree with these authors' statements? Why or why not?
	• Stigler and Hiebert (1999) state that there are six principles for gradual, measurable improvement in mathematics education: expect improvement to be continual, gradual, and incremental; maintain a focus on student learning goals; focus on teaching, not teachers; make improvements in the context of classrooms; make improvement the work of teachers; and build a system that can learn from its own experience. How do you feel that the initiatives outlined in these two articles can help these principles become reality? *(Note to presenter: You may want to divide teachers into groups so each group discusses one principle and reports back on what they discussed about the principle and how the articles support it.)*
	• Stigler and Hiebert argue: "The star teachers of the 21st century will be those who work together to infuse the best ideas into standard practice. They will be teachers who collaborate to build a system that has the goal of improving students' learning in the 'average' classroom, who work to gradually improve standard classroom practices. In a true profession, the wisdom of the profession's members finds its way into the most common methods. The best that we know becomes the standard way of doing something. The star teachers of the 21st century will be teachers who work every day to improve teaching—not only their own but that of the whole profession." (1999, p. 79) What are your thoughts and feelings about this? How does Catherine Lewis's description of research lessons support the development of star teachers?

Activity 2 Understanding Lesson Study	
Purpose	To provide participants with an in-depth overview of lesson study and familiarize them with the lesson study process. Before conducting their own lesson study, participants should thoroughly understand what the process entails, and this section is designed to give this overview.
Materials Needed	• MathStar lesson study process handout (http://mathstar.nmsu.edu/lesson_study/lsdocs/lsprocess.html) • MathStar lesson study process videoclips (http://mathstar.nmsu.edu/Movies/LS5/index.html) Look at: Developing an Overarching Goal; Forming Lesson Study Groups; Designing a Research Lesson; Observing and Debriefing; Reflecting and Revising; and Sharing Findings. • Lesson study process notecards (each table should have six notecards with one of the six lesson study process components on each). **The facilitator should make these notecards in advance.**
Estimated Activity Time	Approximately 30 to 45 minutes for reading overview, watching videoclip examples, discussing components of the lesson study process, and answering questions.
Steps for Facilitation	1. Pass out MathStar lesson study process handout. 2. Have participants read Step 1 of handout and then show the Developing an Overarching Goal and Forming Lesson Study Groups videoclips. Remind teachers that the goal of this activity is to provide them with an overview of the process. Answer any general questions about Step 1. 3. Have participants read Step 2 and Step 3 and then show Designing a Research Lesson videoclip. Answer any general questions about these steps. 4. Have participants read Step 4 and Step 5 and then show Observing and Debriefing and Reflecting and Revising videoclips. Answer any general questions about these steps. 5. Have participants read Step 6 and then show Sharing Findings video clip. Answer any general questions about this step. 6. Ask teachers to work in groups to put the components of the lesson study process notecards in the correct order. 7. Answer any final questions regarding the lesson study process.

Chapter 3: Assessing Your Readiness for Lesson Study

The activity below addresses the integration of process standards in teaching. Professional developers have found that a focus on the processes needed to solve mathematics problems is important for improving student achievement. This activity is placed in the Resources, since many states do not focus on process standards. This is an example. Feel free to adapt this to your own state standards, or to national standards.

Activity 3 Understanding Process Standards	
Purpose	To reflect on the purpose and meaning of the process standards (Problem Solving, Reasoning and Proof, Communication, Connections, and Reasoning and Proof) and share ideas about how they can best be incorporated into classroom practice. This activity also helps participants learn how students' understandings of processes such as problem solving, reasoning, and communication can be assessed both in the classroom and through state-mandated testing.
Materials Needed	• Chart paper. • Markers. • Copies of your state's process standards. • Handout: sample test items from fourth and/or eighth grade. • Handout: scoring sheets for test items. • Transparencies or PowerPoint of discussion questions.
Estimated Activity Time	60 minutes
Steps for Facilitation	1. What are the top three or four concepts in a subject (math, science, and so on) that your students need to know? Ask teachers to think about their students and decide what are the most important three or four subject ideas that they want their students to definitely know during the year. You could ask them to pretend they can only teach three or four main ideas per grade level. Another way to do this is to ask

(Continued)

(Continued)

<table>
<tr><td colspan="2" align="center">**Activity 3**
Understanding Process Standards</td></tr>
<tr>
<td></td>
<td>

teachers what they would want their students to remember from their class if they met them in the grocery store a few years later. Ask teachers to write these on a piece of paper. Share in the group and select the top four items that everyone thinks are essential. As a whole group, list the key ideas from each group to post on the wall (15 minutes).

2. Process standards jigsaw: Each table will read a different process standard (problem solving, reasoning, communication, representation, and connections) and discuss how the process should play out in the classroom.
   - *What does it look like for students and teachers?*
   - *How do the process standards relate to your "big ideas" about content learning?*

Summarize each standard as a whole group (45 minutes).

3. Consider the question:
   - *How do we assess students' development of the process standards?*

Ask participants to share ideas as a whole group for a few minutes.

4. Now, we are going to look at a sample item from the new test so we can see how changes in testing might relate to the process standards. Discuss how the new test will include performance tasks that assess student problem solving skills and communication skills. Let participants know that in order to better understand the types of test items to prepare for, they will solve a sample test item.

5. Do an assessment task (10 minutes to solve the problem, then 15 to discuss as a group). Ask teachers to think about and discuss in groups:
   - *What process skills do students need to solve the problem thoroughly?*
   - *What types of instructional activities should we design to develop process standards skills?*

6. As a whole, summarize the mathematics process and content standards addressed in the test item and the implications for classroom instruction.

</td>
</tr>
</table>

Questions for Discussion

- What do the process standards look like for students and teachers in the classroom?
- How do the process standards relate to your "big ideas" about mathematics learning?
- How do we assess students' development of the process standards?
- What process skills do students need to solve the problem thoroughly?
- What type of instructional activities should we design to develop process standards skills?

Activity 4 Mapping the Standards Against What Is Taught	
Purpose	The previous section was designed for teachers to understand the process standards and what they mean for classroom instruction and assessment. This section is designed for teachers to compare standards to what is actually taught in their program. This is different from the curriculum planning, which is more comprehensive and extends the basic concepts covered in Section 1. The next activity compares this standards map to individual school data.
Materials Needed	• Copies of appropriate state standards, broken out by grade level. • Copies of coding guidelines. • Pink, yellow, and green highlighters, one set per participant. • Transparencies of standards and coding guidelines for demonstration.
Estimated Activity Time	45 minutes
Steps for Facilitation	1. Choose a content strand for use as an example (e.g., algebra). 2. Have teachers get into grade-level groups and brainstorm the "big ideas" for the strand—e.g., what is crucial for kids to know about algebra in sixth grade to be successful—and share their ideas (e.g., on chart paper and posted for the group to see). 3. Pass out appropriate copies of content strand standards and coding guidelines to each grade-level group and explain the

(Continued)

(Continued)

<table>
<tr>
<td colspan="2" align="center">**Activity 4**
Mapping the Standards Against What Is Taught</td>
</tr>
<tr>
<td></td>
<td>

coding process. It may be useful at this point to use the transparencies to model what they will be doing.

4. At this point teachers can be in grade-level groups. They should code their items and make a summary chart of their results for sharing with the group.

5. Discussion of results:
   a. Grade-level groups share their results.
   b. How did what you thought compare to what the standards say?
   c. What kinds of things can this data tell us? (use highlighting and number coding).
   d. Are there gaps in what content is being taught compared to what content the standards say should be taught in this strand?
   e. What are the process standards we are focusing on? Are there process standards that are missing?
   f. What are the implications for our math program?

</td>
</tr>
</table>

Standards and Benchmarks Coding Guidelines

Highlighting Codes for Time on Topic

No Highlighting = **None**, not covered

Light gray = **Slight coverage** (less than one class/lesson)

Medium gray = **Moderate coverage** (one to five classes/lessons)

Dark gray = **Sustained coverage** (more than five classes/ lessons)

Another way to help teachers reflect on how they are covering standards is to help them consider not only how much time is spent on the standard, but how deep this coverage is. Here is another chart that can be used for working with the standards.

Response Codes for Expectations for Students in Mathematics

0 = No emphasis (not a goal for this process standard).

1 = Slight emphasis (less than 25 percent of time on this process standard).

2 = *Moderate emphasis* (25 percent to 33 percent of time on this process standard).

3 = *Sustained emphasis* (more than 33 percent of time on this process standard).

Memorize

Facts

Definitions, terms

Formulas, procedures

Understand and Communicate Concepts

- Explain, define, or represent concepts.
- Apply concepts in procedures and problems.
- Explain procedures, algorithms, solutions, and strategies.
- Develop/explain relationships between concepts.
- Show or explain relationships between models, diagrams, or other representations.

Perform Procedures

- Use numbers to count, order, denote.
- Do computational procedures or algorithms.
- Follow procedures/instructions.
- Solve equations/formulas/routine word problems.
- Organize or display data.
- Read or produce graphs and tables.
- Execute geometric constructions.

Analyze, Reason, Prove

- Analyze or interpret data.
- Write formal or informal proofs.
- Recognize, generate, or create patterns.
- Make generalizations or predictions.
- Identify faulty arguments or misrepresentations of data.
- Reason inductively or deductively.

Solve Novel Problems and Integrate

- Nonroutine problems for which students do not have a routine strategy or algorithm.
- Design a statistical experiment to study a problem.

- Apply mathematics in real-world situations or to other disciplines.
- Generate, extend, or restate problems.
- Synthesize content and ideas from several sources.

<table>
<tr><td colspan="2" align="center">**Activity 5**
Curriculum Analysis</td></tr>
<tr>
<td>**Purpose**</td>
<td>The intended outcome of this section is for teachers to have the ability to evaluate curriculum materials in terms of how well they support high-level teaching and learning. To achieve this goal, teachers will have the opportunity to analyze their own curriculum, and they will also be exposed to various other curriculums so that they are able to identify which curriculum best supports standards-based instruction. Teachers will finish the day by developing a curriculum unit that can be used to fill a gap in their current curriculum.</td>
</tr>
<tr>
<td>**Materials Needed**</td>
<td>

- Copies of appropriate content standards, broken out by grade level.
- Copy of current textbook used in school.
- Copies of reform curriculum textbooks appropriate for grade level.
- Laptops or access to computer and printer for facilitator and each teacher. (If a computer is not available for each teacher, at least have one available for every two or three teachers so that they can work in small groups.)

</td>
</tr>
<tr>
<td>**Estimated Activity Time**</td>
<td>1 day</td>
</tr>
<tr>
<td>**Steps for Facilitation**</td>
<td>

1. Welcome and introductions. Go over purpose of workshop (10 minutes).
2. Pass out a copy of the process standards and the appropriate content standards. Review the process standards and the content standards from the previous workshops (30 minutes).
3. Brainstorm what key elements the teachers like to see in a textbook (30 minutes).
4. As groups, develop an evaluation tool that incorporates the process standards, the content standards, and the key elements identified in Step 2 (30 minutes).
5. Take a break and print the evaluation tool to be used for Steps 5–7 (15 minutes).

</td>
</tr>
</table>

Activity 5 **Curriculum Analysis**	

	6. Have teachers select a "typical" section from their textbook for review. Have the teachers use the tool developed in Step 3 (30 minutes). 7. Pass out a textbook from one of the reform curriculums and have teachers evaluate a section with the tool developed in Step 3 (30 minutes). 8. In small groups, have teachers discuss the differences between their current text and the new textbook (15 minutes). 9. Have a group discussion about which textbook supports thinking and learning better (30 minutes). 10. Identify next steps: How will teachers use this information when textbook adoption comes up for the following school year? (10 minutes). 11. Lunch break (1 hour). 12. List the gaps in the curriculum that were identified in sections 3 and 4 (30 minutes). 13. Have teachers review the new textbook to see if these gaps are filled (30 minutes). 14. Discuss the fact that one textbook will most likely not be matched perfectly with the standards (10 minutes). 15. Break (15 minutes). 16. In small groups, have teachers develop lessons/units that can be used to fill a gap in their curriculum (1 hour). 17. Have teachers present their lessons/units to the group. Print units or provide digital copies for all teachers to take back to their classrooms (30 minutes). 18. Closure and evaluation (15 minutes).

Chapter 4: Connecting Instructional Goals to Lesson Study

The following is a design guideline for giving a basic workshop related to how units are planned. Teachers are encouraged to design their research lessons based on the larger understandings and assessments created around a unit topic.

Part I: Teaching for Understanding

Introduce the notion of understanding by design as a process in which teachers are asked to participate in a three-stage method for developing a unit or lesson.

First, they must identify the enduring understanding they wish students to gain because of having learned the planned topic.

Second, teachers must consider how they can assess or evaluate students to recognize whether or not students understand the key concepts. The second day might include developing pre- and post-assessments for the students they will be teaching, as well as considering assessment strategies to use each day of the lessons.

Third, the teachers will develop the learning activities to be used to help students reach deep understanding of a topic.

Materials needed: Unit plan handout, Essential Questions handout, Establishing Curricular Priorities handout, additional reading material from the Wiggins and McTighe (1998) book *Understanding by Design*.

A. Warm-up Activity

What is understanding?

Ask teachers to work in small groups to explore their own perspectives on what understanding is. Present each teacher with the following three questions to consider individually and write individual answers. After providing time for individual writing and thinking, facilitate group sharing on each question as suggested below:

1. What do you understand really well? Think about something that you are confident that you understand very well. It can be something you do at home, at work, or as part of recreation or play. After individuals have had a chance to think about this, have them share it in a group. The group should make a list and share with the larger group if there is time.

2. How did you get or develop that understanding? Think about and then share your answers to this question. The coordinator can share some answers reported by other groups including: telling someone about it, doing something, feeling success, talking to experts, comparing, using trial and error, doing experiments, reading about this, trying things out, and so on.

3. How do you know you really understand? How do you know how well you understand? Once again, think about what

you understand really well and ask yourself how you know you really understand something. How would someone else know that you really understand this? Share with your small group and with the larger group. Ask the larger group to look at the lists people have generated. What do these lists seem to have in common? What similarities can you find in these lists to what we do in schools? What differences stand out?

Additional Information: The group should come to some agreements about what deep understanding might look like. A definition from the Teaching for Understanding Project at Harvard defines understanding as follows: "Understanding is the ability to think and act flexibly with what one knows." To put it another way, an understanding of a topic is a "flexible performance capability" with emphasis on the word *flexible.* Learning deeply requires more than memorization. It requires applying what is already known to new and unfamiliar situations. Wiggins and McTighe (1998) suggest six facets of understanding that help teachers to think more about understanding. These facets are explanation, interpretation, application, perspective, empathy, and self-assessment. More information about these can be obtained from their Web site (www.ubdexchange.org). You can ask teachers, when they design unit plans, to create assessments in as many of these facets of understanding as possible and then share these assessment activities.

Part II: Enduring Understanding

After thinking about understanding, the coordinator models the idea of enduring understanding in relationship to a lesson. Next, deep understanding is modeled with several topics that might be used by the group. For each topic, ask teachers to pull up relevant content standards and then connect the notion of "big idea" in the standards with students' enduring understanding.

Filters for Determining the Importance of Topics

Both programs for teaching for understanding suggest criteria for selecting topics that lead to the opportunity for students to gain deep understanding. Wiggins and McTighe (1998) suggest four filters to apply to your topic selection.

Filter One: To what extent does the idea, topic, or process represent a "big idea" having enduring value beyond the classroom?

Filter Two: To what extent does the idea, topic, or process reside at the heart of the discipline?

Filter Three: To what extent does the idea, topic, or process require uncovering?

Filter Four: To what extend does the idea, topic, or process offer potential for engaging students?

Essential Questions

Throughout this book, we discuss the importance of questions. As part of planning a unit and research lesson, teachers will need to think about questions that elicit understanding and learning for students. Questions are critical tools for teaching and learning. The essential question for teachers in this exercise might be:

How can I improve student understanding of the content I teach?

or

How can I decide what is most important for students to learn?

Part III: Understanding and Using Essential Questions

The next step is to introduce the idea of essential questions related to enduring understanding. A guide to essential questions was developed by the MathStar project and is shared below. This guide was also used with permission from Intel's Teach to the Future Project to help students plan units around deep understanding.

Guide To Essential Questions

These are key questions that help to focus the learning.

What is an essential question? Questions that probe for deeper meaning and set the stage for further questioning foster the development of critical thinking skills and higher-order capabilities such as problem solving and understanding complex systems. A good essential question is the principal component of designing inquiry-based learning.

What constitutes a good essential question? In general, the best essential questions center around major issues, problems, concerns, interests, or themes relevant to students' lives and to their communities. Good essential questions are open-ended, nonjudgmental, meaningful, and purposeful, with emotive force and intellectual bite, and invite an exploration of ideas. Good essential questions encourage collaboration among students, teachers, and the community, and integrate technology to support the learning process.

How do we write good essential questions? First, consider the focus of the unit or lesson activity. Ideas for a good essential question may stem from your students' particular interests in a topic ("What makes a video game good?"); community resources ("How does pollution impact the Rio Grande River?"); local curriculum expectations ("Who was a great leader in our state's history?"); or a topic suggested by the standards themselves ("Where do waves come from?"). Then, examine the theme or concept in the curriculum that must be addressed and brainstorm questions that you or the students believe would cause them to think about the concept, but without dictating the direction or outcome of their thinking. (For example, the question "Why is fighting bad?" contains its own answer, namely that fighting is bad.) Finally, utilize the six typical queries that newspaper articles address: Who? What? Where? When? Why? and How? and add the word "good" in front of the theme or concept.

How do guiding questions assist the learner? Once an essential question has been identified and agreed upon by the learners, the next step might be to formulate a list of related questions that will assist the learner in answering the essential question. Often embedded within an essential question are subcategories that will generate questions that guide the learner's inquiry. For example, the essential question "What makes a video game good?" might lead to subcategories such as graphics, ease of use, violence, and audience appropriateness, and their subsequent questions. (For example, "How do graphics affect the quality of the game?" or "How does ease of use contribute to its overall rating?")

At the end of this activity, teachers should be asked to read about essential questions and come back the next day with essential questions for their unit plans. Questioning is key to the lesson study process, and questioning and facilitating questioning at deeper levels is a recurring theme throughout this book. It is for this reason that we are introducing questioning and the notion of essential questions in this chapter on planning for instruction.

Practical Note: You can see how this one workshop can be divided into perhaps two or three learning sessions. It could also be provided over two half days. Please feel free to take these ideas and organize them in other ways as your situation requires. The same holds true for all our developed activities.

Resource B

A Problem-Centered Unit

Chapter 5: A Problem-Centered Science Unit

At the beginning of each unit, Susan Brown introduced the problem, provided questions, and facilitated student formulation of questions and hypotheses. Second, she provided resources, mini-lectures, and demonstrations to ensure that students had an adequate knowledge base for solving the problem. Then she provided time for students to move through the centers, reflect on their work, and meet with her for additional questions and discussion. One of the centers was a teacher conferencing space. This is where she made sure that the students understood the science content. She asked them to explain to her what they observed and what they did. Students were then asked to present their findings, and the class and the teacher helped them to evaluate their solutions. Finally the teacher helped the students to make connections and deepen their understanding of how the digestive system works.

Introducing the Problem

The Sierra Sub Sandwich, like most of the units, begins with an opening scenario designed to engage students in the topic to be studied, which in this case is the human digestive system. (This is often called the "hook" by lesson study practitioners and is part of the launch phase of a research lesson.) This is the opening scenario for students to read and have read to them for this unit. In this classroom, the scenario is also read in Spanish.

Sierra Sub Sandwich

Let me introduce myself. I am the Sierra Sub Sandwich. Most people have thoroughly enjoyed my brothers and sisters. To let you know me better, I guess I should describe myself. I am a foot-long white bun with ham, salami, lettuce, onions, olives, mayonnaise, a touch of mustard, pickles, and tomatoes. I always go out with a 9-ounce package of potato chips and a 16-ounce Pepsi. Now, here is what I would like from you! I would like to know beforehand what is going to happen to me when I am eaten. To save me a lot of worry, please write a story about what will happen to me when you order and begin to eat. Your story should include an on-the-spot report of what happens at each part of the alimentary canal that I will be traveling. I realize that I will not all be digested at the same time. I know that different parts of the digestive system will take care of different parts of me. Please let me know which part of me I will lose first. Just tell me!

Also, make the report long and thorough. Please take the time to look up the alimentary canal and describe the parts of what enzymes will be attacking me at what time. Time, time . . . how long will I have in your digestive tract before I am completely gone?

I would also like to know the good that I am doing for your body. Please make a chart listing the calories, vitamins, and minerals that I am contributing to your body.

A picture of my trip would be nice. If possible, please draw a picture, with labels of course, of your alimentary canal. I do not want to make any wrong turns.

Finally, how many calories are you allowed for your age and height and frame? What percent is this meal of your total calories for the day?

Thank you for taking the time to tell me the truth. I will feel better knowing that I am contributing to your healthy, growing body!

Clarifying the Questions and Setting the Framework for Learning

After presenting this scenario, there is much discussion about how to meet the sandwich's request. Lists are made of what students know, want to know, and learn. Questions are asked and clarified.

Videos and Web sites related to the study of the human body are introduced, along with all the center activities. Students work in peer reading groups with relevant sections of the text and begin to write about their ideas and predictions and draw pictures and tables about the project in their science notebooks. The centers are all introduced to the whole class before Susan divides the students into hetero- geneous work groups of four. She is careful to ensure that students who are new to English have a partner who is also a second language learner, as well as two partners fluent in English, but maybe not as skilled in math or computer operation or some other skill as the non-English speakers. This describes the second stage of problem- centered learning, in which the teacher ensures that students con- struct an adequate knowledge base to work on the problem in their small groups.

The Exploration: Providing Students Time to Work on Carefully Structured Tasks Related to the Problem

During the exploration phase, students are provided with time and resources to further understand the digestive system and the prop- erties of different kinds of foods. In this example, sample tasks might include:

- Using iodine to test for the foods that contain vitamin C.
- Testing for fats using foods and a brown paper bag.
- Reading cereal nutrition labels to compare nutrients in different cereals.
- Drawing and/or building the digestive system.
- Comparing the digestive systems of different animals.
- Estimating and creating graphs of calories contained in differ- ent foods.

During this time, the teacher frequently interacts with small groups of students and asks questions about their work. Sometimes they ask questions and want quick answers, but this teacher is care- ful to ask them how they might find out and to guide them to answer- ing the questions themselves. She also checks to make sure that they are writing in their science journals about what they have learned and want to learn.

She has given them an activity to do at home as well. The activity involves reading the labels of the foods they like with their families and answering questions such as: "Which foods contain minerals such as calcium, potassium, or iron or vitamins including A, B, C, D, and K?" During the first week of the project, she holds an all-class meeting to discuss what the middle school children found out about food nutrients from their homework.

Sharing: Helping Students to Design Their Presentations and Evaluate Their Answers

After the students finish their center activities, they return with their group to a large table workspace to design their report and/or presentation for the Sierra Sub Sandwich. Each group answers the following questions, as well as questions they generated, and prepares a multimedia report. They can use not only print but also the PowerPoint program they have all learned, as well as graphs and charts generated with the Excel spreadsheet program they know how to use. If students have the skills, they can also design their own Web page or WebQuest. Students are reminded that the report must include the following items:

1. A story that will describe what happens to the sandwich. Where does each part of the sandwich get digested?

2. An estimation, supported by charts and drawings, of how long the sandwich's parts will be in each part of the digestive system.

3. A chart that shows what nutrients (vitamins, minerals, protein, fats, water, and carbohydrates) are in each of the items that makes up the sandwich.

4. A picture or three-dimensional representation of the alimentary canal with all parts labeled correctly.

5. An estimation of the number of calories contained in the sandwich and what percentage of calories are provided by the sandwich in terms of the daily requirements of calories needed by each member of the group.

As students assemble their presentations, Susan Brown meets with them to evaluate their solutions and their group problem-solving processes. She helps them reflect back on their process of learning, helping them to develop metacognitive skills and self-directed learning skills. The students have kept individual science journals throughout the class, and she also goes over the journals and asks additional questions, extending their thinking whenever possible.

Closure

A teacher familiar with problem-centered learning notices how groups of students are answering the questions and carefully picks groups to share their answers in ways that help the whole group to begin to understand the key concepts being taught. By the end of the unit, the teacher makes sure that the students not only understand the digestive system but can also explain and demonstrate their understanding.

Observation Guidelines

The data that observers collect is an integral part of the research lesson process and should be driven by what it is the research group wants to know. Data collection should be tied to their long-term goals for students, as well as to their specific research lesson goals.

Prior to the observation, each observer should read through the lesson plan developed by the research group. The lesson can be downloaded from the MathStar Web site once it has been submitted by the lesson study group. The observers should take note of the mathematical focus of the lesson and the sequence of activities the teacher and students will be engaged in during the lesson. They should participate in a Web chat prior to observing the research lesson, and be sure they have a clear understanding of what it is they are expected to observe and how and why they are being asked to make the needed kinds of focused observations.

Observers should not interfere with the process of the lesson. They should not help students with the problem or give clarifying instructions to the students. The lesson should flow as if the observers were not present in the room. All observers should plan to participate in the debriefing session and be able to provide a neat, organized, detailed summary of the data that they have collected. This data and the conversation that surrounds it will then help the research lesson team to reflect upon, revise, and summarize what they have learned via their lesson study.

Catherine Lewis has suggested that there are often research goals pertaining to academic/intellectual understanding, to students' motivation to the lesson, and/or to students' social behavior during the lesson. The key is that the focus should be driven by what it is the research group wants to know and by what constitutes good data for answering their questions. If this is done, then there is lots of specific evidence that can be discussed in relation to how well the research lesson met the goals of the lesson.

There may be only one research focus during the research lesson, or there may be more than one. For instance, if teachers have a goal of having students actively engaged in their own learning and they design a research lesson that they hope will meet this goal, they should discuss what constitutes evidence of engagement. They might look for verbal, tactile, and kinesthetic evidence of engagement. Other examples of data to be collected could be: Are students participating by discussing and answering questions? Are students actively problem solving, writing down ideas and solutions? Are students leaning forward and bright-eyed?

There may be one main goal, and each observer may want to focus on a group of students and gather evidence about them. One observer may want to write down numbers of students from the class who participate. The teachers may be interested in a close look at what one student does during the lesson. Maybe there are other things the research group wants to investigate. One observer may focus on engagement and another might focus on understanding.

The bottom line again is that the data to be collected should be driven by what it is the research team wants to know. During lesson study planning, before the facilitation of the research lesson, there should be explicit discussion of what kinds of data will help the research team gather evidence in regard to what they hope to accomplish from their research lesson. These goals should be communicated as specific data that observers should look for and notate.

A final observation example comes from our 2002 summer conference. Our core teachers collaboratively discussed observation criteria related to the main topics area of academics, motivation, social behavior, and student attitudes for the "cube lesson." This is what they came up with.

Academic

- Are they using the vocabulary correctly?
- Is there understanding of the math content?
- Are they actively demonstrating and explaining within their group? How? What are they saying and doing?

Motivation

- How many times are their hands raised?
- Are they asking questions of each other?
- Are they asking questions of the teacher?
- Are they answering questions?
- What types of body language do you observe? (shining eyes, "aha!" comments)

Social Behavior

- What is the frequency of interaction? (How many times do students refer to and build on classmates' comments?)
- Is everyone valuing peer input? How or how not?
- Are students friendly and respectful?
- Is everyone participating?

Student Attitudes Toward Lesson

- What did you like most about the lesson? Why?
- What did you like least about the lesson? Why?

Debriefing Guidelines

One way to begin this meeting is to look back at your research question and then the process you used in the designing a lesson related to the question.

Design: What was the planned learning for students?

Content: What was the concept you wanted students to learn? What evidence do you have of their understanding or lack of understanding?

Environment: What discourse was planned, and what kind of communication occurred? How did the physical environment support or hinder the lesson? What tools were available? What was the emotional climate in the classroom? (Our observation tool relates to these kinds of questions, and having the observer sketch the room would be helpful.)

Hopefully, the data gathered by the observers, as well as your own experiences in doing the lesson, will help answer these questions.

Chapter 5: Additional Professional Development Materials

Lesson Study Final Report Guidelines

Final Report Guidelines

These guidelines provide an overview of the types of questions that we would like teachers from participating lesson study teams to discuss and reflect upon. All research reports should be written in complete sentences and paragraphs and be understandable by educators who have not seen the lesson before, and should cover the following areas: mathematics learning, instructional strategies, and the lesson study process. These areas should explicitly be incorporated into data collection activities during the observation cycle of the lesson study process. Answers to each section should be supported by data that have been collected during observation and discussed during reflection and revision meetings.

Introduction

What is the research lesson topic you investigated this semester? How does this topic relate to the overarching goals for your students and your school? How did you go about planning for this lesson? What resources did you utilize? What is the mathematical focus of the lesson? (What do you want students to know and be able to do as a result of the lesson?) Why did you choose to focus on this mathematical area? What enduring understandings to you hope to help your students gain through this lesson study? Please describe your students (demographics, motivation, learning challenges, and so on).

Curricula Subject Learning

What have you learned about the way different students learn the subject content that your lesson study topic investigated? What does robust understanding of this topic look like?

1. What concepts have students been working with prior to the lesson? What previous knowledge will the lesson build from? What extensions to this lesson would you like to share?

2. What misconceptions or knowledge gaps do students have regarding this concept? How do you know? (Please include examples of student work and adjustments you have made to the lesson plan and/or recommendations you have to help other teachers prepare to address these misconceptions. You may create a detailed list of student misconceptions on a separate sheet of paper instead of within the lesson plan itself, if space is an issue.)

3. How do you ensure that students have gained the mathematical understandings for which this lesson is designed?

4. Summarize any understandings you have developed regarding students' mathematical learning (specific to this concept and in general) as a result of your involvement in this research lesson.

5. What did you learn about this mathematics content? How did you ensure that you had a strong conceptual understanding of this topic?

Instructional Strategies

1. How are the instructional strategies of the lesson designed to build students' understanding of the mathematics concepts listed above? (e.g., what techniques did you use to make sharing of strategies useful and productive?)

2. What changes were made in the lesson from one iteration to the next? Why were these changes made? (Please include a summary of the development of the lesson toward the final form, highlighting why changes were made based on what you learned about the teaching and learning of this lesson.)

3. How did you engage students' interest and attention to the lesson? How did you sustain their minds-on engagement during the course of the lesson? How did you facilitate communication and collaboration during the lesson? How did you assess what your students knew and understood during the lesson? How did you put closure on the lesson?

4. Summarize any understandings you have developed regarding instructional strategies (specific to this concept

(Continued)

(Continued)

and in general) as a result of your involvement in this research lesson. Please reflect upon, summarize, and include examples of what you have learned about classroom communication (e.g., how to foster it through instructional design and/or how to facilitate it via the types of questions that are asked).

Lesson Study Process

1. How has your lesson study team's involvement in the lesson study process impacted the way you work with other teachers at your school?

2. Personally, how did lesson study support your growth as a teacher?

3. What are the strengths and weaknesses of the lesson study process? In what general ways can the lesson study process be improved? How can the lesson study process be adapted to better fit within the context of your school? What recommendations do you have for integrating lesson study into your school schedule?

The processes and documents described above were significantly influenced by the work of James Stigler and James Hiebert, authors of *The Teaching Gap*, and workshop materials from Clea Fernandez and the Lesson Study Research Group. These processes and materials are continuously evolving as we adjust them to the unique needs and challenges of the teachers, students, and educational environment.

SOURCE: From the Mathstar.nmsu.edu Web site; used with permission.

References

Black, P., & William, D. (1998). Assessment and classroom learning. *Assessment and Education, 5*(1), 7–75.

Branson, J., Brown, A., & Cocking, R. (Eds.). (1999). *How people learn.* Washington, DC: National Academy Press.

Butler-Pascoe, M., & Wiburg, K. (2003). *Technology and teaching English language learners.* Boston: Allyn & Bacon.

Cohen, D. K., & Hill, H. C. (2001). *Learning policy: When state educational reform works.* New Haven, CT: Yale University Press.

Connolly, F., & Clandinin, J. (1992). Teacher as curriculum maker. In P. Jackson (Ed.), *Handbook of research on curriculum.* New York: Macmillan.

Darling-Hammond, L., & Sykes, G. (Eds.). (1999). *Teaching as the learning profession: Handbook of policy and practice.* San Francisco: Jossey-Bass.

Deal, T. E. (1990). Healing our schools. In A. Lieberman (Ed.), *Schools as collaborative cultures: Creating the future now.* London, UK: Falmer Press.

Delisle, R. (1997). *How to use problem-based learning in the classroom.* Alexandria, VA: ASCD.

Eisner, E. W. (1994). *The educational imagination: On the design and evaluation of school programs.* Basingstoke, UK: Palgrave Macmillan.

Fenstermacher, G. (1994). The knower and the known: The nature of knowledge in research on teaching. *Review of Research in Education, 20,* 3–56.

Fernandez, C. (2003). Learning from Japanese approaches to professional development: The case of lesson study. *Journal of Teacher Education, 53*(5), 393–405.

Fernandez, C., Cannon, J., & Chokshi, S. (2003). A U.S.-Japan lesson study collaboration reveals critical lenses for examining practice. *Teaching and Teacher Education, 19*(2), 171–185.

Fernandez, C. and Chokshi, S. (2002). A practical guide to translating lesson study for a U.S. setting. *Phi Delta Kappan, 84*(2), 128–134.

Fernandez, C., Chokshi, S., Cannon, J., & Yoshida, M., (2002). Learning about lesson study in the United States. In E. Beauchamp (Ed.), *New and old voices on Japanese education.* Armonk, NY: M. E. Sharpe.

Fernandez, C., & Yoshida, M. (2000). *Lesson study as a model for improving teaching: Insights, challenges, and a vision for the future.* Paper prepared for Wingspread 2000 Conference. Reprinted in *Eye of the storm: Promising practices for improving instruction.* Findings from the Wingspread Conference. Washington, DC: Council for Basic Education.

Fernandez, C., & Yoshida, M. (2004). *Lesson study: A Japanese approach to improving mathematics teaching and learning.* London, UK: Erlbaum.

Fosnot, C. T. (1996). *Constuctivism: Theory, perspectives, and practice.* New York: Teachers College, Columbia University.

Franke, M., Fennema, E., Carpenter, T., Ansell, E., & Behrend, J. (1998). Understanding teachers' self-sustaining, generative change in the context of professional development. *Teaching and Teacher Education, 14*(1), 67–80.

Gollub, J., Bertenthal, M., Labov, J., & Curtis, P. (Eds.). (2002). *Learning and understanding.* Washington, DC: National Academy Press.

Hassel, C. A. (2004). Can diversity extend way of knowing? Engaging in cross-cultural paradigms. *Journal of Extension, 42*(2), 1–4, http://www.joe.org/joe/2004april/a7.shtml

Hiebert, J., & Stigler, J. W. (2004). A world of difference: Classrooms abroad provide lessons in teaching math and science. *JSD, (25)*4, http://www.nsdc.org/library/publications/jsd/hiebert254.cfm

Ingersoll, R. M. (2003). *Who controls teachers' work? Power and accountability in America's schools.* Cambridge, MA: Harvard University Press.

Jacobs, H. H. (Ed.). (2004). *Getting results with curriculum mapping.* Alexandria, VA: ASCD.

Jordan, J., Mendro, R., & Weerasinghe, D. (1997, July). *Teacher effects on longitudinal student achievement.* Paper presented at the CREATE annual meeting, Indianapolis, IN.

Joyce, B., & Weil, M. (1996). *Models of teaching.* Boston: Allyn & Bacon.

Kardos, S. M., Johnson, S. M., Peske, H. G., Kauffman, D., & Liu, E. (2001, April). Counting on colleagues: New teachers encounter the professional cultures of their schools. *Educational Administration Quarterly.*

Kedro, M. J. (2004). *Aligning resources for student outcomes: School-based steps to success.* Lanham, MD: Scarecrow Education.

Killion, J. (2002). *Assessing impact: Evaluating staff development.* Oxford, OH: National Staff Development Council.

Kinzer, C. (2005). *Mathematics and lesson study* (Dissertation). New Mexico State University. Curriculum and Instruction.

Lampert, M. (1998). Studying teaching as a thinking practice. In J. Greeno & S. Goldman (Eds.), *Thinking practices in mathematics and science learning* (pp. 53–78). Mahwah, NJ: Erlbaum.

Lewis, C. (1995). *Educating hearts and minds: Reflections on Japanese preschool and elementary education.* New York: Cambridge University Press.

Lewis, C. (2002). *Lesson study: A handbook of teacher-led instructional improvement.* Philadelphia: Research for Better Schools.

Lewis, C., & Tsuchida, I. (1997). Planned educational change in Japan: The case of elementary science instruction. *Journal of Educational Policy, 12*(5), 313–331.

Lewis, C., & Tsuchida, I. (1998). A lesson is like a swiftly flowing river: Research lessons and the improvement of Japanese education. *American Educator, 22*(4), 12–17 & 50–52.

Lipsey, M., & Wilson, D. (1993). The efficacy of psychological, educational and behavioral treatment: Confirmation from meta-analysis. *American Psychologist, 48*(12), 1181–1209.

Love, N. (2002). *Using data/getting results: A practical guide for school improvement in mathematics and science.* Norwood, MA: Christopher-Gordon.

Ma, L. (1999). *Knowing and teaching elementary mathematics: Teachers understanding of fundamental mathematics in China and the U.S.* Mahwah, NJ: Erlbaum.

Marlowe, B., & Page, M. (1998). *Creating and sustaining the constructivist classroom.* Thousand Oaks, CA: Corwin Press.

Mathematics Learning Study Committee. In J. Kilpatrick, J. Swafford, & B. Findell (Eds.), *Lesson Study, New Mexico Style.* Center for Education; Division of Behavioral and Social Sciences and Education. Washington, DC: National Academy Press.

Mooney, C. (2005). *Theories of childhood: An introduction to Dewey, Montessori, Erikson, Piaget, and Vygotsky.* Upper Saddle River, NJ: Prentice Hall.

National Assessment of Educational Progress. (2003). *Nation's report card: Mathematic Highlights 2003.* (NCES Publication 2004–451). Jessup, MD: U.S. Department of Education.

National Assessment of Educational Progress. (2004). *The condition of education in brief, 2004.* (NCES Publication 2004–76). Washington, DC: U.S. Department of Education.

National Center for Education Statistics. (1999a). *TIMSS: Overview and key findings across grade levels.* (NCES 1999–081). Washington, DC: U.S. Government Printing Office.

National Center for Education Statistics. (1999b). *Predicting the need for newly hired teachers in the United States to 2008–09.* (NCES 1999–026). Washington, DC: U.S. Government Printing Office.

National Council of Teachers of Mathematics. (2000). *Principles and standards for school mathematics.* Reston, VA: Author.

National Research Council. (2001a). *Adding it up: Helping children learn mathematics.* Washington, DC: National Academy Press.

National Research Council (2001b). In J. Bransford, A. Brown, and R. Cocking (Eds.), *How people learn: Brain, mind, experience, and school.* Washington, DC: National Academy Press.

Newsome, J. (2001). *Examining pedagogical content knowledge: The construct and its implications for science education.* New York: Springer.

Norton, P., & Wiburg, K. M. (2002). *Teaching with technology,* Second Edition. Orlando, FL: Harcourt Brace. (Original work published 1998)

Phillips, D. (2000). *Constructivism in education: Opinions and second opinions on controversial issues.* Chicago: The National Society for the Study of Education.

Piaget, J. (1997). *The child's conception of the world.* London, UK: Routledge.

Rivkin, S., Hanushek, E., & Kain, J. (2002). *Teachers, schools, and academic achievement* (Working Paper Number 6691). Cambridge, MA.

Roy, P., & Hord, S. M. (2004). Innovation configurations: Chart a measured course toward change. *JSD, (25)*2, http://www.nsdc.org/library/publications/jsd/roy252.cfm

Russo, C. (2003). *Reutter's the law of education.* New York: Foundation Press.

Sagor, R. (1992). *How to conduct collaborative action research.* Alexandria, VA: ASCD.

Sagor, R. (2000). *Guiding school improvement with action research.* Alexandria, VA: ASCD.

Sagor, R. (2004). *Action research guidebook: A four-step process for educators and school teams.* Thousand Oaks, CA: Corwin Press.

Schmoker, M. (1999). *The results fieldbook: Practical strategies from dramatically improved schools.* Alexandria, VA: ASCD.

Schoenfeld, A. H. (1999). The core, the canon, and the development of research skills. In E. C. Lagemann & L. S. Shulman (Eds.), *Issues in educational research: Problems and possibilities.* San Francisco: Jossey-Bass.

Schools and Staffing Survey. (2000). Retrieved February 1, 2006, from http://webapp.icpsr.umich.edu/cocoon/IAED-SERIES/00098.xml

Shulman, L. (1987). Knowledge and teaching: Foundation of the new reform. *Harvard Educational Review, 57*(1), 2–17.

Sparks, D. (2004). *Leading for results: Transforming, teaching, learning, and relationships in schools.* Oxford, OH: National Staff Development Council.

Stigler, J. W., & Hiebert, J. (1999). *The teaching gap: Best ideas from the world's teachers for improving education in the classroom.* New York: Summit Books.

Stigler, J. W., & Hiebert, J. (2004, February). Improving mathematics teaching. *Educational Leadership, 61*(5), 12–17.

Takahashi, A. (2000). Current trends and issues in lesson study in Japan and the United States. *Journal of Japan Society of Mathematical Education, 82*(12:49–6), 15–21.

Takahashi, A. (2004). Personal communication.

TIMMS. (2003). In I. V. S. Mullis, M. O. Martin, E. J. Gonzalez, & S. J. Chrostowski (Eds.), *Findings from IEA's Trends in International Mathematics and Science Study at the fourth and eighth grades.* Chestnut Hill, MA: TIMMS & PIRLS International Study Center, Boston College.

Wenglinsky, H. (2004). Facts or critical thinking skills? *Education Leadership, 62*(1), 32–35.

Wexford, Inc. (2003a). *Creating change tool.* Retrieved January 30, 2004, from http://www.wexford.org/wexford_files/CreateChangeTool.pdf

Wexford, Inc. (2003b). MathStar Teacher Interviews, June 2002.

Wexford, Inc. (2003c). *Sustaining change tool.* Retrieved January 30, 2004, from http://www.wexford.org/wexford_files/SustainChangeTool.pdf

Wexford, Inc. (2004). *Framework for designing and implementing effective professional development.* Available at http://wexford.org/evidence/ProfDev.pdf

Wiburg, K. (2005). *Student outcomes study, annual report.* (Funding for the Gadsden Mathematics Initiative provided by the National Science Foundation's Local Systemic Change Initiative, #0096674)

Wiburg, K., & Fernandez, M. T. (1993). The effect of one logo learning environment on students' cognitive abilities. In D. L. Watt & M. L. Watt (Eds.), *New paradigms in classroom research on logo learning.* Eugene, OR: International Society for Technology in Education.

Wiggins, G., & McTighe, J. (1998). *Understanding by design.* Alexandria, VA: ASCD.

Wiggins, G., & McTighe, J. (2001). *Understanding by design,* Second Edition. Upper Saddle River, NJ: Prentice Hall.

Yoshida, M. (1999). *Lesson study: A case study of a Japanese approach to improving instruction.* Doctoral dissertation, University of Chicago Department of Human Development.

Index